A TIME TO CELEBRATE

A TIME TO CELEBRATE
Let Us Keep the Feast

JAMES T. FARMER III
Foreword by JENNA BUSH HAGER

Photographs by KRISTEN SCOTT
& EMILY J. FOLLOWILL

Keep the Feast

GIBBS SMITH
TO ENRICH AND INSPIRE HUMANKIND

15 16 17 18 19   5 4 3 2 1

Published by
Gibbs Smith
P.O. Box 667
Layton, Utah 84041

1.800.835.4993 orders
www.gibbs-smith.com

Designed by Sheryl Dickert
Page production by Melissa Dymock
Printed and bound in China

Gibbs Smith books are printed on either recycled, 100% post-consumer
waste, FSC-certified papers or on paper produced from sustainable PEFC-
certified forest/controlled wood source. Learn more at www.pefc.org.

Library of Congress Cataloging-in-Publication Data

Farmer, James T., III.
A time to celebrate : let us keep the feast / James T. Farmer, III ; foreword by Jenna
Bush Hager ; photographs by Kristen Scott & Emily J. Followill. — First edition.
    pages cm
Includes index.
ISBN 978-1-4236-3866-7
1. Cooking, American—Southern style. 2. Holiday cooking.
I. Scott, Kristen. II. Followill, Emily J. III. Title.
TX715.2.S68F369 2015
641.5975—dc23
2015014564

I was taught to celebrate life's accomplishments—no matter how great or small—but to celebrate with love. I also learned to celebrate the humble and proud moments with dignity and grace. Yet, I further learned that these moments were not mine alone, for life's moments were mine to share with family and friends, to celebrate their lives and shower them with love, honoring their times of triumph and their times of joy. All this I learned from my mother, Jeanie Granade Farmer.

With the utmost love, I dedicate this book to Mama—to her memory and to her love for her family and friends. Her love for us knew no bounds, and may we ever live—and love—to the depths she did. She learned it from her mother, my Mimi. What a legacy to uphold! Thank you, Mama—I love you!

Let us Continue the Feast!

Contents

Foreword

Throughout the following pages, my dear friend James Farmer writes of how entertaining is so ingrained in us as Southerners, that entertaining has truly become the backbone of our heritage and a calling card of "Southern Hospitality." Even a Texas gal can identify with that!

James and I share a special bond that has brought us together in many ways over the years. From our ties as Editors-at-Large at *Southern Living* and our paths crossing at the *Today* show, to being raised by graceful, beautiful Southern women, we have developed a genuine friendship, mutually cherishing our families and celebrating with them.

Something James and I also share is the common belief that as Southerners, we have an inherent knowledge of entertaining, and the urge to execute that knowledge that's more than skin deep—it's running deep in our veins. To echo James's sentiments throughout this book, "We get it from our mamas, who got it from their mamas." And mine is no exception.

As First Lady, my mother personified a natural entertainer and brought a healthy dose of Southern hospitality and Texas spirit to the White House too. Whether it was entertaining foreign dignitaries or a quiet family supper in the residence, she taught us how to bring people together at the dinner table with her graceful nature and elegant poise—making everyone from prime ministers to my sister and me feel "at home" in the White House.

From inaugural balls and campaign rallies to weddings and Christmas parties, excuses for a celebration were plentiful in the White House, and I learned quickly by watching and paying attention as my mother executed these events with ease. My wedding on the Ranch was no exception, as a celebration at home has a more momentous feel to it, especially as I return there with my husband and daughter. Having that special connection to the land is a legacy I share with my father and grandfather, and I hope to gift that to my children as well.

Celebrations take on new meanings as we get older. They evolve from sweet sixteens and weddings to baby showers and first birthdays. They serve as a reminder to us of just how cyclical life is, and how every moment should be treasured and celebrated.

James is a refreshing voice in our generation and reminds us of the importance in finding the time to celebrate—even the littlest of life's events. And, of course, adding a little Texas style and Southern flare never hurt! Here's to finding a time to celebrate—each and every day!

—JENNA BUSH HAGER

Introduction

We Southerners simply delight at the opportunity to throw a party, for we can treat any occasion as a celebration! I wholeheartedly believe that our ability to celebrate is part of our hospitable disposition and reputation. My sympathy goes out to other geographic locales not automatically associated with the word "hospitality."

Truly, y'all, I believe one of our proudest moments in history was saving the city of Savannah from Sherman's fiery campaign—a testament to Southerners celebrating for any cause! Besides ingeniously inebriating the Union Army with Chatham Artillery Punch (a blend of liquors that'll knock any army off its boots), Savannah citizens simply did what they knew best—they hosted a party for the invading army. Why would an invasion be a cause for celebration? Well, for one thing, the city was spared from the blaze of war and lives on to this day as the jewel of Georgia's coast. Call it a bizarre form of self-preservation, but it worked. Sherman gave President Lincoln the lovely city of Savannah as a gift rather than a torched and ruined token of war.

A celebration of any sort lights a fire in our bellies to "fluff" around the house. One must polish grandmother's silver, "borrow" flowers from obliging neighbors (or cemeteries—shhh, don't tell), cut the crust off the cucumber sandwiches and roll out enough cheese straws to feed Pharaoh's army—not to mention making enough chicken salad and pimento cheese

for said army. Whether someone is getting married or buried, y'all, we serve chicken salad.

"Fluff" is a very technical term we use in the design business as well. I relish whenever a client calls to say they need a little fluff before a party. Trust me, I know that means this client's home needs a couple more pillows on the sofa, flowers in any julep cup not being used, a couple of urns with flamboyant ferns billowing forth their fronds and a pair of lamps for the buffet. Who knows, I may even sneak in an Oushak rug for the dining room while I'm at it!

Weddings, showers, birthdays, retirements and life's many other milestones and seasonal splendors all lend themselves as reasons to celebrate. Even the luxury of a Sunday evening at home with family—and friends who we think of as family—can be a cause for celebration. In fact, I love the simplicity of a dinner with friends as much as an oyster roast for a hundred folks. These events may be grand or humble, planned or spontaneous, tradition-filled or newly christened, yet they all contain a thread of joy. This joyous thread ordains each event as genuine and heartfelt and ties back to our reputation—after all, Southern hospitality is our calling card!

I can feel the mantle of responsibility from generations before me whenever I entertain. A Southern mantra for life—but especially for entertaining—is "that's the way Mama did it." Our mamas and mamas'

mamas before them have set a precedent and tradition for each generation, hopefully to be preserved and handed down for those to come. Though twists on traditions keep them fresh, it is our familial duty, privilege and honor to continue celebrating our history and heritage. The celebration of heritage is not a particularly unique element to Southern society, by any means, but how our mamas did it—food, flowers, venues and menus—set a tone of reverence for our traditions.

We collect china, crystal, linens and silver from our ancestors and treasure them, for we Southerners are simply stewards of our history. We go weak in the knees when it comes to silver. We even lose our honey-tongued eloquence and talk like we've stuffed our mouths with cotton when it comes to "silvuh." Especially if it is "muhthuhs silvuh suhvice," then y'all know we lose control of our verbal skills and cannot pronounce an "R" to save our hides. Londoners may have their silver vaults, but any Southerner worth their grits will know multigenerational "silvuh" patterns "What's your pattern?" may be followed by "Hello, my name is . . ."

Our genetics give us not only eye color but also prowess for entertaining. Now, we don't all share that gene for entertaining, just as we don't all share the same eye color, but there is a natural inclination to celebrate, especially with charm, style and thoughtful execution. So when it comes to parties, we Southerners simply "do" them. We do the flowers and do the food; we carry out the tasks at hand as if they're second nature. I loved watching how effortless it seemed for my grandmother, Mimi, to feed family and friends on Sundays after church—and how *joyfully* she did so. Mimi, as did the generations before her, prepared a meal gracefully, and thus set the standard and established a tradition. Each generation is bestowed with the responsibility to continue tradition—whether or not your silver pattern matches your grandmother's.

For me, a celebration is a time to cherish the memories of our loved ones, honoring their lives by living ours to the fullest. Making each moment, milestone and event a true celebration is the highest praise to honor a life well lived. I, along with so many of my fellow Southerners, have been given the gift of a life shaped by those before me—those who lived and *loved* wholeheartedly. To have been influenced by my mother, grandmother and a multitude of Southern hosts and hostesses is a treasured gift indeed. It is my privilege to honor this inheritance and celebrate life's happenings each and every chance I can.

So I invite y'all to celebrate with me. Let us celebrate birthdays, weddings, showers, parties and occasions of all sorts. What better time is there to celebrate than now? What better time to rejoice in the life we have been given and treasure those who have celebrated before us? May we ever "keep the feast" with "sincerity and truth" and find a time to celebrate each and every day.

Driving Club Wedding

The famous last words from this Farmer to his pals TJ and Catherine upon news of their engagement: "William and Kate had trees. Y'all will have trees."

When these dear friends asked me to be a part of their wedding, I was truly flattered and immediately began scheming about the décor for the January date. The Schutze-designed Piedmont Driving Club ballroom was the perfect setting for this bride and groom. Catherine grew up in Atlanta proper and TJ's business is based there. The couple is as classic and Southern as the Driving Club itself, and I knew the décor had to be apropos.

The design challenge I faced was how to transform the Piedmont Driving Club into the winter wonderland of Catherine's dreams combined with refined Southern elegance, style, and a classic manner—all while channeling the royal wedding. Enter the trees.

The ballroom is a fretwork of plaster and moldings, sinewy arches and fluted columns—quite reminiscent of a tree with its trunk and branches. I had the ballroom lined with trees lightly adorned with twinkling lights, thus framing the room as in an allée or tree-lined park. A similar effect was used at Westminster Abbey for the Duke and Duchess of Cambridge, and it was perfect for our Southern belle and her beau.

The uplighting on the trees cast leafy shadows across the gently barrel-vaulted ceiling, as if a mural of leaves and stars were in a fresco above us. David Austen roses, white French hydrangeas, green cymbidium orchids and boughs of garden greenery adorned the altar, ballroom and tables—classic style and Southern charm in perfect cadence!

For the menu, we kept with the Driving Club's noteworthy pairings. Two items, in particular, are culinary hallmarks of the PDC: butter crackers and vichyssoise. Rounding out the spread were beef tenderloins, shrimp cocktail, crudités and a wedding cake surrounded by garden roses yielding their sweet perfume.

They say good friends and good wine get better with time, and I am ever so grateful to be in Catherine and TJ's vintage! I hope y'all enjoy this Driving Club–inspired menu. Classics truly never go out of style!

MENU

Classic Cream Cheese
Appetizer with Mascarpone

Driving Club Crackers

Classic Caesar Salad
with Garlicky Croutons

The Farmer's
Homemade Mayonnaise

Vinegary Shrimp Cocktail

Smoked Beef Tenderloin

The Farmer's Vichyssoise

CLASSIC CREAM CHEESE APPETIZER WITH MASCARPONE

Serves 6 to 8

Many a Southern appetizer involves a block of cream cheese. It is a building block—a cornerstone of cuisine! Whether they are topped with pepper jelly or adorned with a myriad of other preserves, cream cheese appetizers will never cease to be en vogue! This version involves mixing in some mascarpone and topping it with your favorite fruit preserves (I really like fig, raspberry, blackberry or strawberry). Serve with ginger snaps for dipping—or scooping and piling it on, if I'm being honest.

---

12 ounces mascarpone cheese

8 ounces cream cheese

1 envelope unflavored gelatin

1 small or medium-size jar fruit preserves

1/4 cup milk or heavy cream

13 pralines

Salted pecans, for garnish

Ginger snaps, for serving

In a large bowl, cream together the mascarpone and cream cheese. Dissolve the gelatin as directed on the package then incorporate well into the cheese mixture.

Line a shallow mold with plastic wrap and fill mold with the cheese mixture. An oval, round, ring or fun shape can be used. Refrigerate the mold for at least 30 minutes to an hour or longer. When the cheese mixture has set, unmold onto a serving platter and spread the top with the preserves.

In a small pot over medium heat, warm the milk. Crumble the pralines into the milk, heating gently until the pralines have melted. Bits of pecan will be visible in the milk mixture. Pour the praline mixture over the molded cheese and preserves, letting it drip and run down the sides. Garnish with salted pecans for that sweet 'n' salty combo that we love so much, and serve with ginger snaps!

DRIVING CLUB CRACKERS

Makes 40 crackers

From stories of chefs at competing clubs sabotaging other chefs' saltines by wetting them, to keeping the true recipe a secret from club members, there is as much legend and lore over this cracker recipe and its history as there are tales of the burning of Atlanta.

When shown to your table at the Driving Club, a linen napkin–lined silver basket is served to you promptly upon being seated. Promptly. The warm crackers are devoured by children, hoarded by "blue hairs" in their clutches and dunked into soup. Regardless of how they are consumed, they are delicious and delectable. This is a version of the famed wetting-and-double-baking style in the tradition of Downtown Atlanta clubs. It has been said that the chefs in these famed institutions wet the saltines, bake them to dry, and then douse them with clarified butter and bake again. Wet and double bake if you desire, but these crackers are divine just as suggested below. And always double the recipe—you'll eat half the batch before you serve them!

---

1 cup (2 sticks) unsalted butter

1 sleeve saltine crackers (about 40 crackers)

Preheat the oven to 400 degrees F.

In a small pot, clarify the butter by melting over low heat and skimming off the white foam. Boil and skim until the butter is clear and golden. This should yield ¾ pound of clarified butter.

Place the crackers in a medium or large bowl and toss with the clarified butter.

Transfer the crackers to a cookie sheet and bake for about 3 minutes. Serve warm!

FARMER'S NOTE: *A dash of garlic salt, Durkee Famous Sauce or Cavender's Greek Seasoning never hurts!*

CLASSIC CAESAR SALAD WITH GARLICKY CROUTONS

Serves 4 to 6

I love a good Caesar salad. Yet I've found that so many versions have been modified or "mayonnaised" beyond the point of recognition. Like good homemade mayo itself (facing), sometimes we must go back to the basics. You need egg yolks for emulsion, sardines for briny brilliance and hearty croutons to soak up any dressing the lettuce leaves behind. In my version of a classic Caesar salad, all the ingredients meld together to form a bold yet light and fresh dish—a short of je ne sais quoi (I do not know what). The Japanese refer to this indescribable flavor combination as "umami." Here's to umami je ne sais quoi, y'all! Oh, the Parmesan? Grate it yourself—it makes a difference.

CAESAR DRESSING

6 anchovy filets in oil, drained

1 small to medium-size clove garlic

Pinch of salt

2 large egg yolks

2 tablespoons freshly squeezed lemon juice, plus more as needed

1 teaspoon good-quality Dijon mustard

2 tablespoons olive oil

1/2 cup vegetable, canola, or other salad oil

3 heaping tablespoons finely grated Parmesan

Salt and freshly cracked black pepper

CROUTONS

3 heaping cups torn rustic country-style bread, crust on

3 heaping tablespoons olive oil

3 heaping tablespoons melted butter

3/4 teaspoon garlic salt

3/4 teaspoon Durkee Famous Sauce, Cavender's Greek Seasoning, or Nature's Seasons

Salt and cracked black pepper

12–18 leaves (2–3 per person) crispy romaine lettuce hearts

Parmesan shavings, for garnish

On a cutting board, chop the anchovy filets with the garlic and pinch of salt. Mash the chopped anchovies and garlic into a paste with your knife, and scrape the paste into a medium-size bowl.

Whisk in the egg yolks, 2 tablespoons lemon juice, and the mustard. Slowly, y'all, drop by drop, add the olive oil and then the vegetable oil, whisking it all together until the dressing is thick, emulsified, and glossy. Whisk in the Parmesan and season to your liking with salt and pepper and lemon juice. (Lemon juice can be used to help thin the dressing too.)

To make the croutons, preheat the oven to between 350 and 375 degrees F. On a baking sheet, spread the torn bread pieces and sprinkle with the olive oil, butter and seasonings; toss to coat. Bake for 10 to 15 minutes, tossing occasionally, until golden.

To assemble the salad, toss the romaine hearts with the dressing and croutons, and garnish with Parmesan shavings.

FARMER'S NOTE: I love to serve a Caesar salad garnished with grilled chicken, fish or shrimp for a meal, but I especially love it with fried okra! Or sometimes I'll mix in some cooked pasta and have a Caesar Pasta Salad!

THE FARMER'S HOMEMADE MAYONNAISE

Makes about 1 cup

Southern mayonnaise is an artistic expression of both devotion and culinary prowess. Mayo can sport a bad reputation with fraudulent recipes and too-sweet mayo-esque spreads and whips. If you have never had homemade Southern-style mayonnaise, you have lived a deprived life. Contributing to the amazing tang and complementary flavors are the egg yolks, which emulsify and make peace between the oil and vinegar.

I could write volumes on homemade mayo, y'all. What you buy at the store just doesn't do justice to the real thing—especially if you're making a 'mater sammich, dipping french fries in it or simply waking up to a good ol' fried egg on toast!

My recipe can easily double as an aïoli if you use only olive oil instead of blending it with canola. I love using olive oil from my friends at Georgia Olive Farms. For the vinegar, I prefer white wine or champagne.

Mimi used to tell me that "some folks are like oil and vinegar—they just don't mix! Some of us have to be the mustard in life."

---

2 large egg yolks

2 tablespoons freshly squeezed lemon juice

1 teaspoon vinegar

1 teaspoon Dijon mustard

1 cup canola oil and good-quality olive oil combined

¼ teaspoon salt

In a medium bowl, whisk the egg yolks together with the lemon juice, vinegar, and mustard. (The mustard is the emulsifier that brings together the oil and vinegar.)

Begin to whisk in the oil one drop at a time. Once the mixture begins to thicken, add the oil more quickly. This is a great exercise in patience! It'll all come together with about 8 minutes of good whisking. You're welcome to use your mixer or food processor, but what's the fun in that? Add the salt in one final whisk.

FARMER'S NOTE: This mayo will keep for a couple of days in the fridge.

VINEGARY SHRIMP COCKTAIL

Serves 3 to 4

Growing up with the Golden Isles of Georgia's coast, the Carolina Lowcountry and the Gulf all within a decent drive of Middle Georgia's farmland, we seemed always to have access to great seafood—especially shrimp, which were Mimi and Mama's favorite.

Mimi and Granddaddy always traveled with a cooler. Peas, corn, blueberries, peaches—and seafood too—always found their way back to our home whenever they journeyed to and from the coast or across SoWeGa (Southwest Georgia, y'all) towards Bainbridge. I am afraid I, too, inherited that trait of toting a cooler. I brake for farm stands, seafood markets and just about anyone selling produce in a roadside tent. What can I say? I was raised right!

Boiling shrimp (and just about anything else) makes them rubbery and tough. I love to steam shrimp (or even have the seafood department at the store do so) and then toss them in a vinegary dressing. Large shrimp work great as a cocktail or passed starter at a dinner party, and this is my go-to way of dressing up some simple steamed shrimp!

Juice of 1 lemon

½ cup white balsamic vinegar

2 teaspoons capers

1 teaspoon caper brine

½ teaspoon dry mustard

Heavy pinch of salt

Heavy pinch of pepper

Heavy pinch of Old Bay seasoning

1 pound large shrimp, steamed, tails removed

Whisk all the ingredients together in a large bowl and toss with the steamed shrimp—preferably while they're still warm. Serve warm or chilled.

FARMER'S NOTE: *For a seasonal nod, make an herb-infused vinegar by adding some basil, tarragon, or rosemary to the vinegar and warming it.*

SMOKED BEEF TENDERLOIN

Serves 20 to 30

Beef tenderloin is a Southern staple of fine parties and events. Having had the great pleasure of touring across the South and attending many a fine party, I have discovered that the secret to the best tenderloins involves how they are treated before and after they are grilled. One party I had the privilege of attending was in St. Francisville, Louisiana, for their Southern Garden Symposium. I had such a good piece of tenderloin that I begged for the recipe—begged to the point that the hostess gave me an entire cookbook full of the recipes of symposiums past! This recipe is my version of the tenderloin from that memorable trip.

Butter and beef make an excellent duo. Whether I'm searing a filet and topping it off with a pat of butter before finishing it in a hot oven or using the butter in a marinade, I feel that this duo is completely apropos—both are gifts from a cow! Ha! I really love this marinade or basting sauce for beef tenderloin, but I also use it with venison, pork and chicken. For pork, I add a heaping tablespoon of honey. Pork pairs so well with the sweet notes of honey, fruit or onions.

I use "pound per person" when serving tenderloin at a sit-down dinner. Half a pound per person is perfect for a cocktail party. Also, be sure to remove the silver skin or tendon from the tenderloin, or ask your butcher to do so. It'll curl up on you while cooking if not removed.

BASTING SAUCE FOR TENDERLOIN

1 cup (2 sticks) butter

3/4 cup good-quality olive oil

2 tablespoons sesame oil

2 tablespoons minced garlic

Juice of 1 1/2 lemons

1 teaspoon liquid smoke

1 teaspoon smoked paprika

3 tablespoons Dale's Steak Seasoning or Moore's Original Marinade

1 tablespoon Cavender's Greek Seasoning

1 tablespoon Lawry's Seasoned Salt

2 tablespoons sesame seeds

10 pounds beef tenderloin

In a small saucepan over medium heat, combine all the sauce ingredients, but do not let the mixture boil.

Marinate the meat in the sauce for at least 2 hours or overnight, reserving about 1 cup for basting on the grill.

On a hot grill, sear the tenderloins on each side for 30 seconds to 1 minute, depending on the size of the tenderloins. This seals in moisture and creates the crust. After searing, move the tenderloins to the side of grill—away from the hottest fire. Cook and liberally baste with reserved marinade until desired internal temperature and doneness is reached. You can even shut off the grill and smoke the meat for a bit for additional flavor.

If you remove the beef when your thermometer indicates rare, you can place the tenderloins in a deep dish or platter and tent with foil. They will continue to cook under the tent for 5 to 10 minutes. Leaving the dish under the smoky grill lid ensures more flavor and smoky essence.

Once cooled, slice and serve. Brush the sliced medallions with a bit of the reserved marinade.

THE FARMER'S VICHYSSOISE

Serves 4 to 6

I can remember the first time Mama took us to the Piedmont Driving Club. For us country mice, a visit to the Driving Club meant we had to mind our Ps and Qs and exercise our most recent cotillion-learned manners. Mama told me many a time that "we may be from the country, but we don't always have to act like it." The Driving Club was no place to show our true country colors.

As we were served our first course that warm day on the terrace overlooking the leafy grandeur of Atlanta's skyline, I vividly recall skimming my soup spoon away from myself and tasting a delicious yet shockingly cold soup! Mama's eyes could warn and wither us in an instant, but they could comfort and ease even faster. This time, she noticed my expression and shock, and without missing a beat she proclaimed, "My, this vichyssoise is as delicious as always!" I instinctively took her cue and realized that this soup was served to me cold on purpose. That the cold soup had a fancy name just made it that much more enchanting to me.

I was enthralled and knew then that one day I would return to the Driving Club and ask the server not for the cold soup, but for a cup of vichyssoise.

Vichyssoise is a French term for a cold potato and leek soup made famous in the dining room of the Ritz hotel in London. While it is delicious on a hot summer day, I also enjoy it warm. It can be a one-pot wonder if you boil rather than roast the potatoes.

4–5 pounds baby Yukon Gold potatoes

Sea salt

Freshly ground black pepper

4 tablespoons olive oil, divided

1–2 tablespoons chopped fresh rosemary

1/4 cup butter

1 large onion, finely chopped

5 cloves garlic, chopped

2 ribs celery, chopped

1 bay leaf

1/2 teaspoon chopped fresh thyme

1 teaspoon Nature's Seasons

1/2 teaspoon celery salt

3 leeks, white and green parts, thoroughly washed and chopped

3 cups chicken stock, divided

2 cups buttermilk

1 cup sour cream

1 cup milk

1/2 cup chopped parsley or green onion, for garnish

Preheat the oven to 425 degrees F. Slice the potatoes in half and place into two roasting pans. Season well with salt, pepper, 2 tablespoons olive oil, and rosemary. Roast the potatoes until golden and beginning to brown.

In a heavy-bottomed Dutch oven, pot, or kettle, heat the butter and the remaining 2 tablespoons oil. Add the onion, garlic, celery, bay leaf, and thyme to the pot, seasoning with Nature's Seasons and celery salt, and cook until lightly browned.

Add the leeks and 1/2 cup chicken stock, and deglaze the bottom of the pan, scraping any browned bits. Add the buttermilk, sour cream, milk, and remaining 1/2 cup chicken stock. Stir until simmering and add the roasted potatoes.

With an immersion blender, puree the soup. A chunkier soup is more rustic, while a thoroughly pureed soup is more elegant. Add more milk to thin or finish off if need be. Chill thoroughly for a true vichyssoise; also delicious warm.

Garnish with parsley before serving.

Mountain Wedding

The Southern summertime heat is like a fever—it either breaks or ultimately gets the best of you. To add insult to injury, the old adage "It's not the heat; it's the humidity . . ." really is more aggravating than informative. The saying should be "It's the heat AND the humidity" that get you exasperated and sweaty beyond comfort and attractiveness. Thank goodness for the mountains, or we would all succumb to feverish heat and reach our permanent wilting point. "I will lift up mine eyes unto the hills, from whence cometh my help." The psalmist was right as rain with that one!

The Appalachian foothills start along the Chattahoochee River Valley, which strides along Georgia and Alabama's border; and even there, just in those foothills, the fever pitch of summer's heat can be evaded. As you crest along the mountainous spine of this ancient range, the temperatures begin to sink as the elevation begins to rise, and you'll find your attitude changing with the altitude. For centuries Southerners have fled the farmlands and lower countryside of the Deep South to revive themselves with the cooler temperatures of an Appalachian summer.

Summer is a glorious season! Leafy green mountains intersect with blue skies unfazed by humidity. A very warm day may reach eighty degrees, and a nighttime fire is not unheard of. From Highlands to Cashiers, Brevard to Asheville and upwards towards Chimney and Blowing Rock, with mountain lakes dotting in between, Southerners from NOLA to Charleston all meander up to the hills for some summer salvation. For many families, cottages, cabins and chalets are generational destinations, and places such as Cedar Mountain, North Carolina, become the meeting place for gaggles of grandparents, grandchildren, parents and cousins.

The mountains are a destination for weddings too, and this topic involves a short introduction of some favorite women in my life. I have three wonderful Maggies. My sister is Maggie—Sarah Margaret proper—and mother to my beloved nephew Napp, making me Uncle Brubbs, my favorite title ever! My childhood best friend is Maggie—Maggie Coody Griffin—and we loved each other so much as children that we've decided to stay best friends forever. Both of these Maggies married beaus from our hometown and good buddies of mine. Yet both of them did something I did not expect—they moved away! God knew I needed a local Maggie and He graciously sent her to me in Perry. What a gift she has been!

When Perry Maggie met our local football coach, Coach Josh, we all knew it was meant to be. One test he had to pass, though, was the mountain test—could he leave the sultry southland of Georgia and escape for a spell to the mossy grandeur of western North Carolina? Of course he could, and did! For this

MENU

Asian-Style
Grilled Chicken

Mountaintop
Potato Salad

Arkansas Green Beans

Steamer's Sauce 2.0

Aunt Martha's
Caramel Cake

Aunt Rhoda's
Pound Cake

Peachy Pink Lemonade

couple, Maggie's familial home outside of Brevard—Cedar Mountain, to be exact—was the perfect spot to get married. Picking a date in July was a stroke of brilliance too, for we could all leave our wilted existences in Middle and South Georgia and celebrate in the mountains!

Though the weekend proved misty and cool, we welcomed the weather as a respite. A chapel boasting centuries of nuptials, services and congregations under its roof was the site for the ceremony. Perched on a ridge, this historic chapel and its mountainous surroundings invoked the season and enveloped the attendees with a sense of delight, comfort and solidarity. For the reception, a pole barn overlooking the valley proved a perfect setting for the celebration.

In the South, barns are twofold in purpose—farm life and parties. It's a natural symbiosis for our agrarian-rooted lifestyle. Plus, our barns are typically bigger than our houses, making them easier places to entertain a hundred or more folks! Rough and quartersawn oak and pine boards formed this barn and reminded us all very quickly of our relationship with the land. Mountain breezes sweetened by hay fern and laurel drifted through the bays. Long tables set family style invited the guests to sit and visit and enjoy the reception.

Mountain wildflowers such as bee balm and Queen Anne's lace filled baskets and jars, while pails of green apples gave a nod to the coming season and the cash crop of this land. Wooden trays from reclaimed timbers boasted their contents as the centerpieces. All the while, twinkling lights cast romantic shadows amidst the lightning bugs darting about and casting their cadence.

Summer's jewels—peaches—found their way onto the menu along with other Southern classics. Green beans, potato salad, pound and caramel cakes, lemonade, and even some North Carolina house wine—otherwise known as moonshine—all filled the guests with comfort and nostalgia of celebrations from days gone by.

As we head to the hills, like our families have done for generations before us, we Southerners value that tradition of returning to our happy places for life's momentous occasions. A mountain wedding to rejuvenate and inspire, while reminding us of our heritage, is just the medicine for a Southern summertime fever. I am so lucky that one of my Maggies knows this remedy too!

ASIAN-STYLE GRILLED CHICKEN

Serves 4 to 6

Chicken and delectable peaches both fare so well on the grill. This is one of my ultimate summer suppers! A simple, savory and quick marinade for the chicken makes it a year-round staple, but the addition of grilled peaches is fantastic. I like to add a bit of peach jam to the marinade and baste the chicken with it, too, for additional flavor. The longer you can marinate the chicken, the better.

4–6 medium to large boneless, skinless chicken breasts

ASIAN-STYLE MARINADE

1 cup soy sauce

1 tablespoon sesame oil

1 tablespoon teriyaki sauce

1 tablespoon minced garlic

1 tablespoon minced ginger

1 tablespoon honey

1 tablespoon peach jam, plus more for basting

Juice of 1 lemon

Pinch of salt

Pinch of freshly ground black pepper

Dry the chicken breasts and set aside.

Whisk together the marinade ingredients and marinate the chicken in the refrigerator for at least 1 hour; overnight is better.

On a warm grill or smoker, grill or smoke the chicken until thoroughly cooked. Baste the chicken with peach jam upon turning. Remove the chicken from the heat and keep warm.

GRILLED PEACHES

Utilize the last heat from the fire to grill the peaches. Their juice will caramelize and create a browned, sugary char.

4 fresh peaches, halved and pitted with skin intact

Freshly squeezed lemon juice

Olive oil

While the coals or grates are still hot, brush the open, pitted half of the peaches with lemon juice and olive oil. Place flesh-side down on the grill. The peaches become tenderer with the heat and can be grilled to your liking. Serve with the grilled chicken, on salads, or as a dessert with ice cream!

MOUNTAINTOP POTATO SALAD

Serves 4 to 6

This potato salad is so delectable you'll think your taste buds have reached the pinnacle of flavor! I love to use baby Dutch yellow potatoes; they are so buttery and tender. Plus, they're baby enough that they need little to no chopping—one less step to prep! This recipe can easily be doubled and the bacon adds a fun flavor! Pancetta and chopped ham work well too.

---

1 pound baby Dutch yellow potatoes

1 cup chopped thick-cut bacon (about 8 slices)

1-2 tablespoons olive oil

Salt and freshly ground black pepper

1 cup mayonnaise

1/2 teaspoon freshly squeezed lemon juice

1/2 teaspoon salt

1/2 teaspoon freshly ground black pepper

1/2 teaspoon paprika

1/4 cup minced fresh parsley, plus more for garnish

2 tablespoons grated onion

1 tablespoon minced fresh chives, plus more for garnish

1/2 teaspoon curry powder

1/2 tablespoon Worcestershire sauce

1 clove garlic, minced

1 tablespoon capers

1 tablespoon caper brine

1 cup sour cream

Preheat the oven to 415 degrees F. Slice any potatoes that are larger than average size to ensure equal roasting.

In a roasting pan, toss the potatoes and bacon in olive oil and season well with salt and pepper. Roast until potatoes are soft and golden brown—some charring is desired—or until the bacon is crispy. This should take about 20 minutes.

In a large bowl, combine all the remaining ingredients for the dressing and mix well. Add the warm potatoes to the bowl and mix with the dressing. Serve warm or chilled. Garnish with additional chopped chives or parsley.

ARKANSAS GREEN BEANS

Serves 10

Leave it to a bunch of Georgians to gather in the North Carolina Mountains and eat Arkansas Green Beans. I've heard many a story as to why this dish is named for said state, and all of them pay homage to the awesome flavor combo it purveys and the ease with which it's prepared.

You can fry, roast or microwave the bacon, but however you cook it, make sure it is crispy! The flavor combo of sweet and salty with crispy and tender is just fantastic, and we won't even mention the heavenly aroma! Fresh green beans work well, too, if blanched, but canned beans and microwaved bacon is just so easy.

---

5 (15-ounce) cans green beans, drained

7–10 slices bacon

2/3 cup firmly packed brown sugar

1/4 cup melted butter

8 teaspoons soy sauce

1 tablespoon chopped garlic

2 teaspoons garlic powder

Preheat the oven to 350 degrees F. Place the green beans in a lightly greased 9 x 13-inch baking pan.

Place the bacon on a microwave-safe plate and microwave for 2 minutes, until slightly cooked. Lay the bacon on top of the green beans.

Combine the brown sugar, butter, soy sauce, chopped garlic, and garlic powder in a small bowl. Pour the butter mixture over the green beans and bacon. Bake uncovered for 40 minutes.

STEAMERS
SAUCE

STEAMER'S SAUCE 2.0

"IF YOUR CHEEKS TWINGE, THEN THE SAUCE IS READY."
—STEVE "STEAMER" JENKINS

Makes 1 quart plus

I wrote about Steamer's Sauce in Dinner on the Grounds *and how Perry Maggie's father, Mr. Steve "Steamer" Jenkins, made it for friends and family. Steamer truly was a memorable man, it was only fitting to have his sauce at Maggie's mountain wedding. A jar of this famous sauce made a memorable token for each guest to take home.*

When Maggie gave me the recipe for Steamer's Sauce, she told me, "This is basically a guideline—you can add or take away according to your taste preferences." I can't improve on it much at all, but I do call this version Steamer's Sauce 2.0. A touch of sweetness from the brown sugar melds wonderfully with the tangy bite of vinegar! Speaking of vinegar, use the store brand if you can; it usually has less sugar.

Mrs. Maggie Jenkins Schuyler also gave this bit of advice: "The way you know it's ready is when you dip white bread into the sauce for a taste, and it makes your jaws twitch. If the smell makes your jaws twitch too, then it positively is ready."

---

1 tablespoon butter

1 tablespoon olive oil

1 medium yellow onion, chopped

2 large cloves garlic, chopped

1 pint store-brand white or apple cider vinegar

1 (14-ounce) bottle yellow mustard

1 (24-ounce) bottle ketchup

2 tablespoons liquid smoke

1–2 teaspoons lemon juice concentrate

$^2/_3$ cup firmly packed brown sugar

Texas Pete hot sauce

Salt and freshly ground black pepper

In a large saucepan over medium heat, heat the butter and olive oil; brown the onion and garlic. The onion can have some caramelization and the garlic can be very brown, just not burnt.

Add a splash of vinegar to help deglaze the pan.

Pour in the remaining vinegar and add the mustard, ketchup, liquid smoke, lemon juice, and brown sugar. Season to taste with hot sauce and salt and pepper. Simmer for about 1 hour, adjusting the flavor as desired.

AUNT MARTHA'S CARAMEL CAKE

Serves 12 to 16

Caramel cakes hold a certain aura of their own in the Southern cake hierarchy. Making caramel can be dictated by the weather and can require using candy thermometers and whisking and watching with the patience of Job. Plus, there is the anatomy of the cake. Should it have thick layers or ultra-thin layers? And should the icing be gritty or smooth? These are questions of great debate that have been known to split a Sunday school class into near-irreparable schisms.

My only caution about caramel cakes is that they tend to be dry—which calls for a thick layer of frosting! Whether the cake has uber-thin layers or is a thicker three-layer version, whether the icing is smooth or a bit gritty, I like them all. But if I had to decide, I might go with a thicker layer and a slightly gritty icing. This combo isn't necessarily the run-of-the-mill Southern-style caramel cake, but it makes me go weak in the knees. When I see that thick, slightly gritty icing atop three thick layers of moist yellow cake, I am a goner—slain at the sight and close to a sugar coma after my third piece. A glass of cold milk is practically a medical necessity.

When talking about caramel cakes to fellow Southern cooks, we are somewhat guarded with our techniques and recipes, and we play our recipe cards close to the vest. But every now and then, you get a talker—and that is when epiphanies on Southern baking come to pass.

At Maggie's wedding, I devoured this amazing caramel cake while talking to her aunts and cousins. I, of course, was prying at every angle to get this recipe and had a moment of near insanity when I didn't get it immediately. I was beginning to think Aunt Martha took it to her grave, especially after umpteen family members at the reception told me there was a secret to the cake but they "just couldn't share it." The consistency reminded me of another cake too, but I couldn't place it. I was stumped with no help from any of Martha's nieces—all of whom did, however, confide that they were her favorite niece.

I was in agony. I knew there was an answer to why this cake was moist yet crumbly and had that thick, gritty icing— that icing that I was scraping off the cake knife upon return for seconds and thirds. Finally, after much dismay and near contempt for the whole family for not sharing the secret, a precious, adorable, sweet, genuinely kind cousin approached me. She said, "Honey, I'll tell you the secret. I know Aunt Martha would've been honored for you to have the recipe. She would've loved you. My cousins probably don't know it, and you simply haven't called their bluff. And, after all, I was her favorite niece." She certainly was my favorite niece right then and forevermore!

Buttermilk and red velvet cake—minus the "red"—were the secrets! Plus, Aunt Martha used Aunt Rhoda's caramel icing recipe. It was as if the heavens opened and manna poured down to feed my body and soul! Buttermilk I know is a Southern staple to ensure a moist, delicious cake, but the absence of red food coloring kept me from recognizing the consistency I almost knew but couldn't put a name to.

After being empowered with such knowledge, I once more broached the recipe topic with the contemptuous cousins and nieces and hinted ever so cunningly that I had the secret. "Well, then, do share the secret!" they all exclaimed and begged and woefully pleaded. I simply said, "Just ask Aunt Martha's favorite niece."

This recipe is for a two-layer cake. If you want to make another, separate batch of batter, you can have three thick layers.

continued>

AUNT MARTHA'S CARAMEL CAKE (CONTINUED)

½ cup shortening

1½ cups sugar

2 eggs, room temperature

2 tablespoons cocoa powder

1 teaspoon salt

1 teaspoon vanilla

2½ cups sifted Swans Down cake flour

1½ teaspoons baking soda

1 teaspoon vinegar

1 cup cultured buttermilk

Aunt Rhoda's Caramel Icing (recipe follows)

Preheat the oven to 350 degrees F. Grease and lightly flour two 9-inch round cake pans.

In a stand mixer, or using a hand mixer in a large bowl, cream together the shortening, sugar, and eggs. Gently add the cocoa to the creamed mixture. Add the salt, vanilla, and flour to the creamed mixture and beat well. I like to add the flour in thirds.

In a separate bowl, mix the baking soda and vinegar together. Gently fold—do not beat—the vinegar mixture and the buttermilk into the cake batter.

Pour batter into the prepared pans. Bake for 30 minutes. (I don't know if this really is the trick, but I will sometimes remove the pans at 29 minutes. No two ovens are the same and that just may be my superstition.) Let the cake layers cool for 5 minutes before removing from pans to cool completely.

When cool, ice the bottom layer, then stack and ice the second layer. Stack the third layer and spread icing on the top and sides.

AUNT RHODA'S CARAMEL ICING

This is a quick fix to an old-fashioned icing and avoids the problem of the sugar burning.

1 pound (2 cups packed) brown sugar

1 (5-ounce) can evaporated milk

¼ cup (½ stick) butter

1 (6-ounce) package butterscotch morsels

In a saucepan over medium-low heat, cook the brown sugar, evaporated milk, and butter until a small ball forms when dropped into cold water. This may take 10 to 15 minutes. Add the butterscotch morsels and beat until melted and well incorporated.

And that, y'all, is the easiest caramel icing! You don't have to use a candy thermometer or have the right humidity or air temperature! Thank you, Aunt Rhoda!

AUNT RHODA'S POUND CAKE

Serves 10 to 12

The South has a few legendary cakes that can make or break a homemaker or host. If they cannot make one of these legendary cakes, then they know who can. That, my friends, is proof that knowledge is power. Red velvet, caramel and coconut cakes are the holy trinity of Southern cakes for special occasions, high holidays and visiting dignitaries. However, pound cakes are the Queen Mother of all Southern cakes for all occasions and take precedence year-round as the cornerstone of Southern baking. If you are married or buried, there will be pound cake.

Mama made me a pound cake every year for my birthday. Without question, it is still my favorite. It is simple and delicious, malleable with the seasons and apropos at any event, celebration, party, nuptial or funeral. A pound cake freezes beautifully, and it can be flavored with citrus, chocolate, cinnamon or fruit. Even the foundation can be varied using whipping cream, sour cream, cream cheese or milk. There are as many pound cake recipes as there are "stars in the Southern sky," and for that I am grateful.

I'm forever thankful my friend Maggie got hitched at Cedar Mountain. Otherwise I wouldn't have Aunt Rhoda's pound cake recipe! Ha!

---

3 cups sugar

1 cup Crisco shortening

1 cup (2 sticks) butter, room temperature

6 eggs

3 ¼ cups all-purpose flour

1 cup milk (I use buttermilk with a splash of milk)

1 tablespoon butternut flavoring

½ teaspoon lemon extract

Preheat the oven to 325 degrees F. Grease and lightly flour a Bundt or pound-cake pan.

In a stand mixer, or using a hand mixer in a large bowl, cream the sugar, Crisco, and butter until fluffy. Add the eggs one at a time, beating continuously. Add the flour, milk, butternut flavoring, and lemon extract; mix well.

Pour the batter into the prepared cake pan and bake for 1 hour and 25 minutes. Allow the cake to cool in the pan for 5 minutes, then remove to cool completely.

PEACHY PINK LEMONADE

Makes 1 gallon plus

Lemonade is such a flexible party drink. It is a fantastic foundation for inserting seasonal flavors or mixing with tea, and it's refreshing simply on its own. I like to use my basic lemonade recipe and then add some of the peachy pink flair for pizzazz, making it festive and fun for a party, reception or shower. Hope y'all enjoy!

THE FARMER'S BASIC LEMONADE

2 cups freshly squeezed lemon juice

1 cup sugar

10 cups warm water

Ice cubes

Sliced lemons or lemon wedges, for garnish and flavor

Whisk together the lemon juice, sugar, and 5 cups warm water until the sugar is well dissolved. Add the remaining 5 cups water and stir. Cool the lemonade with 1 or 2 cups ice cubes and garnish with lemon slices or wedges.

For the peachy pink flair, make a separate batch of lemonade using a store-bought pink lemonade packet. Follow the directions accordingly, mix with my basic lemonade, and garnish with raspberries, strawberries and peaches!

Farmer's Note: Peachy Pink Lemonade can have a dash of moonshine, vodka, or rum.

Lowcountry Boil

The fretwork of marshes and tidal rivers lacing the South Carolina landscape from slightly north of Charleston to the Savannah River are collectively known as the Lowcountry. From this genesis springs forth Southern cuisine, with a depth and breadth that reaches beyond the marshes and into hearts and homes throughout the South.

"Frogmore Stew" or "Beaufort Stew" or a "Lowcountry Boil"—whatever you call it, this one-pot feast of shrimp, sausage, potatoes, corn and onions has been gathering families and friends for generations. The first two titles are of historic provenance, while the latter is more of a regional style. In true Southern custom, this dish has a Cajun cousin known as bouillabaisse and an Italian American cousin, cioppino. However, a Lowcountry Boil is drained from its liquid and served atop a table (usually clad in newspaper) rather than over rice or as a stew proper.

For us in the midlands of Georgia—where the sandy loam of South Georgia and the red clay soil of Middle Georgia collide—we are nearly equidistant to the Lowcountry of South Carolina, Savannah and the Marshes of Glynn as we are to the Gulf. Thankfully we're close enough to the Lowcountry to have adopted some of its cuisine. My family has entertained with a Lowcountry boil for as long as I can remember. Mimi, my maternal grandmother, pronounced the word *shrimp* in her native South Georgia tongue—and as many in her generation did, with the "s" and the "r"

together more so than the "shr" combo: "We're having ssssrimp for supper tonight." Southerners have a way with words, and dropping the sounds of certain letters makes us memorable.

Having hosted and attended many a Lowcountry boil, I started to realize that something was not completely complementary in the cooking fashion of this dish. The sausage was often boiled to a rubbery texture, the potatoes had no flavor and fell apart, the ssssrimp were curled beyond repair and difficult to peel, and the corn might as well have been a sponge—soft and full of water. So I endeavored into a dangerous pastime—thinking. It hit me that boiling all these ingredients together is easy and efficient, but it can be their demise as well. My thinking led to an idea for a party and to try a new recipe on a few of my friends—well a hundred or so of my friends, but a gaggle of folks nonetheless. I would host a Lowcountry *Broil*!

After their wedding in the mountains, Maggie and Coach Josh returned to Perry and we hosted this Lowcountry Broil together out at my family's pavilion. This pavilion has been the scene for reunions, wedding receptions, engagement parties, birthdays and barbeques and was prime for a Lowcountry boil–style party.

I firmly believe that smoke and fire are the finest cooking methods around. Using their heat for broiling, grilling, smoking, roasting and baking have been the hallmarks of cooking since time began. I wanted to

MENU

The Farmer's Lowcountry
Boil and Broil

Broiled Barbeque Shrimp

Sweet Tea Sangria

Mini Crab Cakes and
Sweet-n-Spicy Rémoulade

Farmer's Summer Salad
with Herbed Vinaigrette

Golden Rice Salad

Sweet Tea Cake
with Lemonade Frosting

Peachy Puddin'
with Whipped Cream

inject the flavors of fire and smoke into what should be a flavor-rich meal. So I decided to combine the boil and broil, dump them on the table, and see what my friends enjoyed.

It wasn't long before we ran out of food. Even the potatoes were being snatched up for seconds and thirds—the potatoes that are usually left behind and picked over! There was not a link of sausage, a kernel of corn or a shrimp—baby or jumbo, for that matter—to be found. I had discovered my favorite new style for a LCB. Here are my conclusions for this method of preparation and presentation:

- Boiling is fine. Just don't overdo it. Throw the shrimp in *last* and only for a couple of minutes. Cooked ssssrimp should be in the shape of "Cs," not "Os," and they are ready once they turn from gray to salmony pink: "C" is for cooked and "O" is for overcooked.

- Grill some of the stars of the show. In fact, grilling the sausage and corn with some onion is a must! The fire and smoke work their magic, and the complementary textures with the boiled potatoes and onions are luscious!

- Be sure your boiling water is well seasoned. And who says it must be water and water alone? Chicken or seafood stock, many different aromatics, and seasonings are essential! Onion, celery and garlic cloves are perfect in the pot!

- Rosemary and Old Bay were made for one another. Trust this Farmer—the combo used in the boil and dusted again upon the finished dish on the table is perfect. The heat will help release the rosemary's essence when it's used as a garnish.

THE FARMER'S LOWCOUNTRY BOIL AND BROIL

Serves 12

4 pounds small red potatoes or baby Dutch yellow potatoes

4 Vidalia, red, or sweet onions, quartered

6 ribs celery with leaves, roughly chopped

3 heads garlic, halved

10 sprigs fresh rosemary, plus more for garnish

2 quarts water

3 quarts chicken or seafood stock

1 (3-ounce) package crab boil seasoning

4 tablespoons Old Bay seasoning, plus more for garnish

2 pounds hot smoked sausage links, cut into 1 1/2-inch pieces

6 ears corn, halved

4 pounds large fresh shrimp, tails on, peeled and deveined optional

Cocktail sauce, Mimi's Sauce*, or Lemon Dill Sauce (recipe follows), for dipping

Lemon wedges, for serving

For a traditional boil, add the potatoes, onions, celery, garlic, and rosemary to a large pot, then add the water, stock, crab boil seasoning, and Old Bay. Cover pot and heat to a rolling boil; cook for 5 minutes. Add the sausage and corn, and return the mixture to a boil. Cook for 8 to 10 minutes, until potatoes are tender. You can even reduce the cooking time for the potatoes and let them rest upon the serving table, where they will continue to cook for about 5 minutes in residual heat.

Better yet, broil, grill, roast, or bake the sausage and corn and then add to the table when serving!

Add the shrimp to the pot and cook for 2 to 4 minutes, until the shrimp turn pink. Drain. Serve on a table topped with newspaper and garnish with Old Bay and fresh rosemary. Serve with cocktail sauce and fresh lemon wedges.

*Mimi's Sauce is a mixture of mayo, ketchup, lemon juice, minced garlic, salt, pepper, and Nature's Seasons.

LEMON DILL SAUCE

I relish this sauce with shrimp, crab or fish. It makes a great addition to seafood dishes as a sauce proper or dip, but it can also be spread on a sandwich or added to salad. Fresh lemon juice and zest is the key, and the kick from mayo and buttermilk is so luscious with seafood! Y'all enjoy!

Makes about 1 1/4 cups

3/4 cup mayonnaise

1/2 cup buttermilk

1 tablespoon sour cream

2 teaspoons freshly squeezed lemon juice

1 tablespoon freshly grated lemon zest

2 small cloves garlic, minced

2 tablespoons chopped fresh dill

1 tablespoon minced fresh parsley

Blend or vigorously whisk together the mayo, buttermilk, and sour cream in a bowl. Add the lemon juice and zest and incorporate well. Mix in the garlic, dill, and parsley. Chill until thickened.

BROILED BARBEQUE SHRIMP

Serves 3 to 4

If you aren't serving a bunch of folks and dumping the main dish down a fifteen-foot table covered in newspaper, this is one of my favorite shrimp dishes. Mimi told me one time that "barbequed" doesn't always mean "a pit of smoke and a whole hog . . . it is a way cooking—like baking or broiling."

I love this dish as a dinner for two, but you can triple it for your supper club or dinner party. If a milder flavor is desired, a dash of soy sauce, a pinch of curry or brown sugar all fare well in place of the hot sauce. Serve this shrimp with a side of grits, Carolina Gold or jasmine rice, or pasta. I'm sure this will become one of your favorite shrimp dishes, too.

---

1 1/2 pounds unshelled shrimp

3–4 ribs celery with leaves,* coarsely chopped

2 cloves garlic, chopped

Juice of 2 lemons

1/4 cup (1/2 stick) butter, cubed

2 tablespoons cracked black pepper or mixture of black, white, and red pepper

1 1/2 tablespoons Worcestershire sauce

1 1/2–2 teaspoons salt

Pinch of paprika

Dash of hot sauce, pepper sauce or Tabasco

Rice, pasta, couscous, farro, or grits, for serving

Lemon wedges, for garnish

Preheat the broiler.

Wash and pat the shrimp dry and place them in a large shallow pan. Add the celery and garlic, squeeze the lemon juice over the top, and dot with butter.

In a small bowl, mix the pepper, Worcestershire sauce, salt, paprika, and hot sauce. Sprinkle the shrimp with the seasoning mixture. (Alternatively, you can dust the shrimp and vegetables with each seasoning individually.)

Place the pan under the broiler until the butter melts and the shrimp begin to turn pink, about 5 minutes. Stir it several times while under the broiler. Watch carefully that it doesn't burn. Once the shrimp are slightly pink, reduce the oven temperature to 350 degrees F and bake for 15 minutes. Serve with rice, pasta, couscous, farro, or grits. Garnish each serving with a lemon wedge.

The leaves add flavor.

SWEET TEA SANGRIA

Serves 12

My friend Megan Brent at the Perfect Pear in downtown Perry is known for her fabulous food, parties, and catering—and for some reason, her Sweet Tea Sangria is present at every event! I think that is her secret—the tea and her delicious crab cakes! Let's just say that any time I have Megan cater a party, her Sweet Tea Sangria is always well received and the secret to some dance moves of near-legendary status in our circle! Megan won't reveal all her culinary and drink secrets, but here is my version. I hope I make you proud, Megan!

The house wine of the South, sweet tea is the base for this "sangria." Taking a batch of Farmer's tea, sun tea, herbal tea or your favorite fruit tea and infusing it with Southern summer fruits makes a gorgeous drink for all. Tangs and sweets, florals and herbals, and aesthetics with delicious tastes all meld together for this drink—perfectly at home on your porch, piazza or veranda. Gather up a group of your favorite people, or just have a solo splurge, and enjoy a glass of Sweet Tea Southern Sangria.

---

1 gallon Farmer's Tea or your favorite tea

4 peaches, pitted and sliced into wedges

4 plums, pitted and sliced into wedges

2 limes, sliced into rounds

2 lemons, sliced into rounds

1 large or 2 small oranges, sliced into rounds

A handful of fresh cherries

A handful of fresh raspberries

A handful of fresh blackberries

1 (750ml) bottle good-quality rosé or white wine, such as pinot grigio or Chardonnay

A splash of mint, rosemary, lavender, or ginger-infused simple syrup to taste (about $1/2$ cup for the whole batch, or served in a small pitcher for individual servings)

In a large pitcher, mix the tea with the sliced and whole fruit. Add the wine and flavored syrup of your liking and stir well. Serve over ice or chilled right out of the fridge. The longer it sits, the more infusion of fruit flavor the tea takes on. The sangria will be good for a couple of days in the refrigerator, but I doubt you'll have much left when your crowd downs this one! Enjoy!

FARMER'S TEA

Makes about a gallon

8-10 cups water, divided

4 tea bags of your choice

1 tea bag Earl Grey

$1 1/2$ cups sugar

2-3 cups water

Bring 6–7 cups of water to a rolling boil. Add 4 bags of Lipton (or whatever brand you prefer) and 1 bag of Earl Grey and remove from heat. Let the tea bags steep for about 5 minutes near the warm eye of the stove.

In a separate saucepan, add sugar to the water (I use a 1:2 ratio) over medium-low heat; stir until sugar is dissolved and the water becomes a somewhat clear syrup.

Combine the steeped tea and simple syrup in a large pitcher, or split between two half-gallon pitchers. If you're using a glass pitcher, be sure to have a metal knife or spoon to pour the tea over so the hot liquid doesn't bust the glass.

Fill the pot with the tea bags in it one more time with water and add that water to the pitcher; you can add a bit more water to suit your taste. Stir with a long knife or spoon.

MINI CRAB CAKES AND SWEET-N-SPICY RÉMOULADE

Makes 4 small crab cakes

To me, crab cakes are an easy dish. They should be cakes of crab with just a slight amount of binding. Too much breading, filler and other seasonings drown out the delicate, sweet and buttery flavor that crab naturally possesses. But crabmeat is expensive, thus I like to make mini crab cakes for an appetizer or to accompany a salad—using ingredients that pair well with the crab. One ingredient I love in crab cakes, potato salad and egg salad is dry mustard. Mustard is such a complementary flavor to crab, and it's also a great vehicle to carry other flavors through. Other good ingredients are herbs that bring out the delicate flavor of the crab with their own subtlety, such as parsley and chervil.

My friend Megan Brent also makes a great crab cake for her parties. They are passed around as a fun starter and gobbled up by all those stalking the servers for more! Another style of crab cakes I love are those at the Buckhead Diner in Atlanta. Thinking of an inland diner with fantastic crab cakes doesn't always conjure up a pleasant image, but let me assure y'all, Buckhead Diner has a mighty fine crab cake. So, in thinking about some of my favorite crab cakes, I had to put together my own recipe. I will gladly be the martyr and be sacrificed to testing crab cakes in order to write a good recipe—somebody must do it, after all!

You can double or triple this recipe as needed. These crab cakes are great to pass around as a starter to any meal, as a topper to a salad or even as a sandwich on toasty bread or a croissant. Of course, you'll need a touch of rémoulade, so I've included a smoky yet sweet recipe with a hint of spice.

---

1 pound fresh jumbo lump crabmeat

1/2 cup finely chopped green onions, including some green tops

1/2 teaspoon finely minced chervil, plus more for garnish

1/3 cup mayonnaise

1 tablespoon Worcestershire sauce

1/2 teaspoon dry mustard

1/2 teaspoon curry powder

1 tablespoon Old Bay seasoning

3 slices white bread, diced

2 tablespoons peanut oil (maybe a tad more)

Parsley, for garnish

Smoky Sweet-n-Spicy Rémoulade (recipe below), for serving

Gently pick through the crabmeat to remove any shells. Be careful not to break the lumps; lump crabmeat is worth its weight in gold! In a medium bowl, combine the crabmeat, green onions, and chervil; stir gently to mix together.

In a small bowl, whisk together the mayonnaise, Worcestershire sauce, dry mustard, curry powder, Old Bay seasoning, and bread; stir until well mixed. Add the mayonnaise mixture to the crab and gently fold everything together.

Heat the peanut oil in a large, heavy-bottomed sauté pan or iron skillet over medium heat. With a soup spoon or wooden spoon, scoop out about 1/2-cup portions of the crab mixture and form into small cakes. Sauté the crab cakes for about 3 minutes per side, or until golden brown and a delicious crust has formed. Add more peanut oil as needed.

Garnish the crab cakes with parsley and serve with rémoulade.

SWEET-N-SPICY RÉMOULADE

Some old-fashioned recipes for rémoulade call for a hard-cooked egg. I've had that version, and it is good. But I don't always have just one egg handy, and if I do have one on hand, I have one dozen for egg salad! Here's my rémoulade that is perfect with crab cakes, delectable with shrimp, and even better with oven fries or roasted potatoes—no egg required! I love anything that is a mélange of flavors, and this has a slightly smoky, sweet and spicy flavor that I really enjoy.

¼ cup chopped fresh parsley, or
   2 tablespoons dried parsley

3 green onions, chopped

2 cups good-quality mayonnaise

¼ cup sugar

¼ cup olive oil

Juice of ½ lemon

1 tablespoon capers

A dash of caper brine

1 tablespoon grated onion

1 tablespoon grated celery

1 tablespoon Creole mustard

¼ teaspoon salt

¼ teaspoon cracked black pepper

¼ teaspoon red pepper

¼ teaspoon liquid smoke

Pinch of paprika

Pinch of garlic salt or Nature's Seasons

Blend all the ingredients together until smooth. Serve with crab cakes or just about anything else!

FARMER'S NOTE: A dab of anchovy paste goes a long way and is quite good in this rémoulade!

FARMER'S SUMMER SALAD WITH HERBED VINAIGRETTE

Serves 8 to 10

There is nothing like a good summer salad. Textural greens mixing with farm-fresh fruit and a dressing with flavors stemming right from the garden—it is an entire season captured within a single dish! I like to serve this salad as a side to a heavy meal or as a meal itself with a piece of grilled chicken, fish or shrimp. I also like to mix it with various fruits and garden flavors any chance I can.

The dressing for this salad makes plenty and can be kept chilled for a week, so make and enjoy it while the warmth of summertime is yielding plenty of tasty flavors from the garden!

---

1 clove garlic, peeled and cracked

4 cups mixed greens, such as baby spinach, arugula, butter lettuce, etc.

2 cups microgreens, such as sunflower greens

1 cup shredded green or red cabbage

3 green onions, chopped, white and green parts

1 cup basil leaves

Sliced fresh peaches, blueberries, and strawberries

HERBED VINAIGRETTE

1 cup good-quality olive oil (sunflower oil, pecan oil, or good old-fashioned salad oil work well too)

$1/4$ cup champagne vinegar

Juice of $1/2$ lemon

1 tablespoon honey

1 tablespoon peach, apricot, or pear nectar or apple cider

$1/4$ teaspoon salt

$1/4$ teaspoon pepper

$1/4$ teaspoon garlic powder

4-5 fresh basil leaves, julienned

Rub down the sides of a large wooden bowl with the garlic clove. Wash and dry the greens and place them in the bowl. The garlic seasons the bowl after continual use and seasons the salad too. I learned this trick from Doe's in Greenville, Mississippi—an ultimate destination in Southern cuisine!

In a Mason jar with a lid, add all the dressing ingredients. Close the lid tightly, shake until well incorporated, and pour the dressing over the salad. Add the fresh fruit and toss!

GOLDEN RICE SALAD

Serves 4 to 6

In 1685, a merchant ship in distress near Charleston Harbor paid for its repairs with a small quantity of rice seed—a special seed from Madagascar. From there, a plantation owner, Dr. Henry Woodward, planted the seed, and thus began a two-hundred-year era of rice growing in South Carolina, which became the leading producer in the United States. Towards the turn of the twentieth century, a weak market for this rice—along with inadequate machinery and growing competition from the Gulf States—led to the end of the South Carolina rice cultivation.

Slowly, small farms and companies such as Carolina Plantation Rice have been cultivating and bringing back to market the authentic "Carolina-grown" Carolina Gold rice. Carolina Gold is a creamy, distinctly flavored rice well suited for risottos, puddings and even salads. I love using this rice as a summer salad, for it is delicious served warm or chilled and scrumptious with fruit and a slight bite from a vinegary dressing.

Not all salad can be served warm or cold, or even at room temperature, but this Golden Rice Salad is one such dish. Golden raisins, halved grapes and a vinaigrette navigate through the creamy rice and fare well together on a warm summer night. This rice is a fantastic base for other seasonal fruits. I really love the complementary components of dried and fresh fruits; hence, the raisins and grapes in this dish. Add a dash of pine nuts, toasted pecans or walnuts for some sweet-and-salty pizzazz and crunch.

This salad proves itself as a soulfully delicious side or even main course. A piece of salmon, a few grilled shrimp, a juicy piece of grilled chicken—each would work ever so well if you'd like to make this side the star!

RICE

4 cups liquid (i.e., 2 cups water and 2 cups chicken stock)

2 cups Carolina Gold rice

2 tablespoons butter

Salt and freshly ground black pepper

Sesame Vinaigrette (below)

1 cup golden or mixed raisins

1 cup green or red grapes, halved

³⁄₄ cup pine nuts, toasted

Fresh mint or basil leaves, for garnish

For the rice, bring the liquid to a boil in a large pot and add the rice. Cover the pot, reduce the heat, and allow the rice and cooking liquid to simmer for 15 to 20 minutes, until the liquid is absorbed and the rice is tender. Always fluff the rice with a fork—a spoon for rice fluffing is not respectable in a Southern kitchen!

Shake all the dressing ingredients together in a lidded Mason jar. Toss the dressing with the cooked rice, add the fruits, nuts, and mint or basil and toss again.

FARMER'S NOTE: *When they're in season, citrus fruits pair really well with all this for some punch. Dried apples and fresh apples are perfect for fall.*

SESAME VINAIGRETTE

1 cup olive, pecan, or salad oil

¹⁄₂ cup sesame oil

1 tablespoon sesame seed

Pinch of salt

Pinch of pepper

²⁄₃ cup rice wine vinegar

Shake all the ingredients together in a lidded Mason jar, and toss dressing to taste with the cooked rice.

SWEET TEA CAKE WITH LEMONADE FROSTING

Serves 16 to 20

I love sweet tea. I love lemonade. I love cake. I love frosting. Need I elaborate? I give this fun Southern classic-in-the-making a twist by using my Earl Grey sweet tea flavored with rosemary or lemon thyme.

---

1 1/2 cups boiling water

3 family-size tea bags plus 1 bag Earl Grey—you'll use a good cup of tea in the recipe

1 small sprig rosemary or 2 stems lemon thyme

1 cup (2 sticks) butter, softened

2 cups granulated sugar

1/2 cup firmly packed light brown sugar

5 large eggs, room temperature

3 1/2 cups cake flour

2 teaspoons baking powder

3/4 teaspoon salt

1/4 teaspoon baking soda

1 cup applesauce

Lemonade Frosting (recipe follows)

Preheat your oven to 350 degrees F. Grease a 9 x 13-inch pan with shortening and dust with flour.

In a heatproof glass bowl, pour the boiling water over the tea bags and sprigs of herbs. Cover with plastic wrap and steep for 10 to 12 minutes. Lift the tea bags and herbs from the liquid. To get all the tea from the bags, press them against the side of the bowl using the back of a spoon. Discard the tea bags and herbs and allow the tea to cool for 20 minutes.

In a separate large bowl, beat the butter at medium speed with an electric mixer until smooth and creamy. Gradually add the granulated and brown sugars, beating until the mixture is light and fluffy. Add the eggs 1 at a time, beating after each addition just until blended.

In a medium mixing bowl, whisk together the cake flour, baking powder, salt, and baking soda. Add the flour mixture to the butter mixture in thirds, alternating with 1/2 cup tea, beginning and ending with flour mixture. Beat the batter at low speed just until blended after each addition. (Discard any remaining tea, or sweeten and enjoy a glass!) Add the applesauce and beat the batter just until blended. Pour the batter into the prepared pan.

Bake for 35 to 40 minutes, or until a wooden pick inserted into the center comes out clean. Cool completely on a wire rack for about 20 minutes. Spread the frosting on the cake.

LEMONADE FROSTING

1 (8-ounce) package cream cheese, softened

1/4 cup (1/2 stick) butter, softened

6 cups powdered sugar

1 tablespoon lemon zest

3 tablespoons freshly squeezed lemon juice

In a large bowl, beat the cream cheese and butter at medium speed with an electric mixer until smooth and creamy. Gradually add the powdered sugar, 1 cup at a time, beating at low speed until well blended after each addition. Slowly mix in the lemon zest and lemon juice just until blended. Increase your mixing speed to high, and beat the frosting until light and fluffy.

FARMER'S NOTE: Bourbon, Vodka or Limoncello add an adult kick to the frosting. A hearty splash (2 to 4 tablespoons) is a gracious plenty.

PEACHY PUDDIN' WITH WHIPPED CREAM

Serves 8 to 10

This dish was born accidentally, but it has become a family favorite. Basically, this is a crustless peach cobbler. The texture is thick and somewhat creamy like a cobbler, but the subtraction of a binding crust makes it a bit runny—like pudding before it is set.

I thought Aunt Kathy was putting the crust on the cobbler. Aunt Kathy thought Meredith was putting the crust on the cobbler. Meredith thought Susie was putting the crust on the cobbler. Susie thought Maggie was putting the crust on the cobbler. Long story short, there were too many cooks in the kitchen and the "cobbler" was baked sans crust.

Rather than adding a crust, we plopped whipped cream and ice cream atop the "cobbler," and no one was the wiser. It has now become a summertime staple for our house. I hope y'all enjoy!

---

3 tablespoons melted butter

1 dozen or so peaches, peeled and sliced

5 tablespoons Minute Tapioca

1 scant cup sugar (depending on the cook's palate and sweetness of the peaches)

2 tablespoons cinnamon

2 teaspoons vanilla extract

Whipped cream or vanilla ice cream, for serving

Preheat your oven to 350 degrees F. Melt the butter while the pan is preheating.

Mix together the peaches, tapioca, sugar, cinnamon, and vanilla in a large bowl and set aside.

Add the peach mixture to a deep casserole or baking dish and bake until golden and bubbly, about 1 hour. If you want it "pretty" for serving, let it rest and cool. If not, dig right in! Peachy Puddin' tastes just fine!

Serve warm with homemade whipped cream or good vanilla ice cream. The cream will melt and make the pudding even yummier!

Grown-Up Birthday Bash

Sometimes when two folks meet, stars align and maybe even a supernova somewhere in space explodes. Immeasurable energy is created, and it must be invested somewhere. That was the case when I met one Miss Jessica Elizabeth Vinson—aka "Gup"—in Hawkinsville, circa . . . well let's just say we were children. Nowadays she is better known as Jess "Frou Frou" Margeson. That supernova channeled its energy into our friendship.

Upon returning indoors from a day of summer fun on our farm, I found my mother propped up on the green and white cabana-stripe wicker chaise in her room. Her toes were drying from a fresh coat of "Cajun Shrimp," which was Mama's color eleven months out of the year. "Big Apple Red" was applied at Christmas, but "Carl" was Mama's favorite color. She wore it well and decorated our home with it too. Other folks may know it as coral, but my family and friends know that "Carl" is the proper Southern pronunciation.

This scenario was not an odd one for my sisters and me to witness. Mama was pretty religious when it came to her nail color. As I passed by her bedroom door, she waved and woo-hooed at me. "I just met the cutest, sweetest, most precious Christian girl. I think y'all should get married. If not, she's gonna be your best friend, I know. I already love her. She liked my nail polish and hair. She's raised right!" That's all it took for Jess to brand herself on Mama's heart.

I was about eleven years old at the time, and an SPCG (the acronym given in my family to gals of such merit) for me to be friends with, let alone marry, was not on my radar. Yet mamas have those inklings and premonitions when it comes to their children. Jess's family had just moved to town and, serendipitously, down the street from us. Fate and destiny are one thing, but nothing could tear asunder what my mama joined together.

Pretty soon, Jess and I were friends. We rode the bus together to our school in the next town and thus had plenty of time to bond. Thereabouts, our nicknames "Gup" and "Doodle" were formed, respectively, as in line with all good friendships boasting nicknames. There are stories to the nicknames, but I shan't digress. We survived middle school together, but when high school came around, Jess moved to the big ol' city of Macon. We kept in touch by phone and met for our dates—donned in overalls—at the Fair. (When you're from my neck of the woods, the Georgia National Fair is simply known as THE Fair. There is no other fair in our minds.) I even abused her GAP employee discount all throughout high school (and into college as well). Those were darker days in our friendship, since a twenty-mile stretch of I-75 separated us. When you cannot drive yourself to or from Macon, that I-75 corridor might as well be the Atlantic.

MENU

Georgia Bellinis

Cornmeal-Crusted
Fried Green Tomatoes

Cocktail Shrimp-n-Grits

Berry Parfait Shooters

Tomato and
Mozzarella Salad

Broccoli-Cheddar Quiche

Margeson Family
Date Nut Cake

Mama June's Carrot Cake

College brought us back together in the same town. Auburn called, and we answered. After announcing to our respective families that we were going to live together, we had to dissolve said scheme and live in proper boys and girls dorms due to the near-coronaries we caused our mamas. We spent practically every moment we could together at Auburn. Our dorms were literally across the street from one another. I even (excuse the bravado and boasting, but this a collegiate accomplishment of great ability at Auburn) was able to sneak past Miss Minnie, the dorm mother, and hide out past curfew in Jess's dorm room. It may have been time by the dormitory's rule book for "gentlemen callers" to leave, but Jess and I were often not through crafting, scheming our next adventure or simply rehashing the same ol' childhood funnies over and over. Somehow, the stories we tell get funnier with age and repetition!

While at college, Jess set her sights on a KA pledge named Matt Margeson. He fit her specific bill for what she was looking for in a man. Matt fit the bill with me because he asked me to "please keep dating Jess" when they got married. "I think it is the only way this will work," he said.

I did the flowers for their wedding (with a 102 temp and the flu, mind you. Hey—what are friends for?), and Jess has accompanied and crafted with me on weddings, parties and events across the South. From Richmond to Montgomery, we've decorated and decked the halls in many a Confederate capital city. Her floral design business, Frou Frou, is based in Opelika, Alabama, so she remains close to the Promised Land—"the rolling plains of Dixie, 'neath the sun-kissed skies."

For her "thirty something" birthday, Jess was inspired by a *Southern Living* collaboration we had recently done in Cashiers. What the two of us can do with a pumpkin is nothing short of magical! Ha! Jess is great at the small stuff and I like the big stuff. I tackled the mantels and entry tables (mainly because I could reach them: I'm six foot four and she's a good five feet and slight change), and she tackled the pumpkin centerpieces. We met in the middle at the table, set it, fluffed the pillows and the job was done! Simpatico defined!

Her party was the soirée of the season in East Alabama! Of course, in true Southern fashion, we planned the event around Auburn's football schedule. Set amid the trees of Oak Bowery—an antebellum plantation house near Opelika—guests were greeted not only by the crisp, cool autumn air but also by the sights, sounds and smells of a fabulous party. Acoustic notes of some of Jess's favorite tunes melodically filled the air from the live musicians. Cocktails of both food (Cocktail Shrimp-n-Grits) and beverage (Georgia Bellinis) greeted the guests upon arrival.

Peach, coral, blush and champagne hues bedecked the guests and menu, and the evening literally glowed in the waning sunlight of autumn and under a harvest moon. Cinderella and heirloom pumpkins in the aforementioned shades were scattered, stacked, and arranged ever so elegantly and even used as centerpieces with blousy drifts of roses, ferns, berries and other autumnal flora.

The guests sat at a long banquet table cloaked by ancient cedars and glowing with candles and lanterns. Having had our fill of Cocktail Shrimp-n-Grits, Cornmeal-Crusted Fried Green Tomatoes and Georgia Bellinis, we then feasted on some of Jess's favorite dishes. Broccoli-Cheddar Quiche was accompanied by a Tomato and Mozzarella Salad, Berry Parfait Shooters and, last but not least, a duo of desserts! Jess' mother-in-law, "Mama Marge," made the legendary Margeson Family Date Nut Cake, and "Mama June" Vinson, Jess's mother, made her fantastic carrot cake.

So very unlike our childhood birthday parties, our grown-up parties are more an extension of businesses—with Bellinis. There is something so sound about doing what you love for a living. Jess and I have found our passions and created professions. We are fortunate that our businesses coincide and that we can collaborate regularly. Work isn't so much "work" as it is a blast of fun, and while it is labor nonetheless, it is a labor of love! But having a friend like Jess, who I've known and loved—and to whom I can rave about how much I love sheet moss—is a prized gift indeed.

GEORGIA BELLINIS

Serves 8 to 10

Jess and I grew up in the peach- and pecan-laden fields of Middle Georgia. Our classmates and friends, who were the children of peach and pecan farmers, are still our friends to this day. During the summertime, when the heat has no seemingly plausible expiration date, a grave thought crosses many a Southerner's mind—the heat may last but the peaches will stop coming in. You can insert "squash," "tomatoes," "okra," "corn," etc., for "peaches" and know that our need to "put up" our produce is fanatical.

In this same vein, there is a deafening, paralyzing, poignant panic that Southerner's feel pulsing through their veins and psyche. It comes from the haunting words of our mamas, mimis, great-aunts and aged church ladies: "If I don't put up these peaches before they rot, we'll have nothing to eat this winter." Again, insert your produce of choice for "peaches" in that phrase. The thought of gaunt Southern children leaning against white columns is terrifying, but no doubt they'll be adorned in ironed seersucker and linen with looping monograms. Some things must not be sacrificed! Ha!

Thankfully, we have modern grocers and access to international produce these days, but the South has a knack for preservation of our foodstuffs. It is a part of our congruence with the land, our surviving through wars and depression; relying on "put ups" for sustenance has been ingrained into our cultural psyche. Before refrigeration and freezing, canning, pickling, smoking and salting were our methods of preserving. These are still wonderful methods of preservation, having become nearly artistic and something of an artisan hobby as well.

Freezing revolutionized Southern households. It brought ice to our tea, ice cream to our cobbler and frost to our julep cups. And it allowed us to traverse our countryside with a cooler to stock up on peas and peaches and shrimp and anything else in season we wished to take home with us. Deep freezers at home became signs of prominence on Southern farms, and I have giggled at the thought of little ol' bitties asking each other, "Well, Louise, what do you have in your deep freezer? Martha Nell and I put up all the peas we could pick." In order to stay in good standing, Louise can only retort, "Well, Sue Ellen, honey, I only have a side of beef, fifteen pounds of sausage, some peaches and a pound cake put up. I hope we have enough."

I have a dear friend who always comes to mind when it comes to deep-freezing Southern foodstuffs. Her freezer is stocked with Virginia country ham, Outer Banks shellfish, Lowcountry rice, Georgia peaches, Brunswick stew, Florida citrus, Gulf seafood and a tub or two of Jambalaya from her summertime treks across the South. I tell her that if anything ever malfunctioned with her freezer, it would be akin to the burning of Atlanta.

So I write all this to say that, more than likely, we all have a bag of frozen peaches in our freezer. You may even be like me and have a freezer-burnt bag or two with your mama's or mimi's handwriting that matches the date and script on the jelly jar in the pantry. What better way to celebrate and honor their thoughtfulness, hard work and legacy?

Champagne or sparkling rosé

Frozen peach puree (recipe follows)

For every bottle of champagne or sparkling rosé, you'll need 2 heaping cups frozen peach puree. Or top each flute of champagne with a dollop of peach puree and celebrate the day! Salut, y'all!

PEACH PUREE

Fresh peaches

Peel your fresh peaches and slice the fruit from the pit. Puree the sliced peaches in a blender or food processor, then transfer to a freezer bag or container. These are good for at least up to 1 year.

CORNMEAL-CRUSTED FRIED GREEN TOMATOES

Serves 4 to 6

Fried green tomatoes are legendary in the South. There are novels and movies by the same name and as many versions and methods as there are pound cakes. This dish has even become tres chic, y'all!

I love the history and reasoning behind the tradition more than the tradition itself. I remember asking Granddaddy—aka Big Napp—why he was picking so many green tomatoes. Weren't we supposed to wait until they were red on the vine? "Well, son, for Mimi to fry, of course."

Often, the summertime produce is so abundant that even the unripe things like green tomatoes are harvested to keep the vine in production. Green tomatoes have a spicy flavor on their own and are wonderful additions to sauces, salsas, pastas, and salads and make good pickles too. At the end of the growing season, when the first frost is nigh, all the green tomatoes will be harvested again and used in the myriad ways this fruit can be enjoyed. A cornmeal crust gives some grit and substance to these tomatoes, and dried herbs that pair so well with the tomato flavor are a great addition to the batter or as a garnish.

---

2 cups vegetable oil for frying, plus more if needed

4 medium to large firm green tomatoes

1 cup buttermilk, plus more if needed

1 egg, beaten

1–2 tablespoons water

Salt and freshly ground black pepper

$\frac{1}{2}$ cup all-purpose flour

1 cup yellow cornmeal

$\frac{1}{4}$ cup panko or finely processed dried bread crumbs

$\frac{1}{8}$ cup finely grated Parmesan cheese

$\frac{1}{2}$ tablespoon dried basil

$\frac{1}{2}$ teaspoon dried oregano

Heat the oil in a cast-iron skillet or Dutch oven to 350 to 375 degrees F. Slice the tomatoes into about $\frac{1}{2}$-inch-thick rounds and pat dry with paper towels.

Whisk together the buttermilk, egg, and a tablespoon or so of water in a shallow bowl or pie pan until well blended. It should be thick but not watery. Just a splash of water helps keep it from getting too thick. A dash of salt and pepper here is good too. This is your "wet" element.

Mix the flour, cornmeal, panko, Parmesan, basil, oregano, and a pinch of salt and pepper together in a shallow dish such as a pie pan. This is your "dry" element for "wet, dry, fry."

Dip the sliced tomatoes in the buttermilk-and-egg mixture, then dredge in the flour-and-cornmeal mixture.

Fry the 'maters for about 2 minutes per side, or until golden brown. If the oil becomes depleted or too cloudy, add more oil and wait until that oil is hot before frying the next batch. Set fried tomatoes on a paper towel–lined plate to drain.

COCKTAIL SHRIMP-N-GRITS

Serves 6 to 12

A twist on the combo dish of shrimp and grits, this version includes a steamed shrimp with cheesy grits—served in a mini martini glass! Shrimp steamed with plenty of Cajun spices pairs perfectly with grainy grits full of cheese and garlic!

CHILLED SPICED SHRIMP

1 1/2 cups apple cider vinegar

1/2 cup water

Juice of 1 lemon

3 cloves garlic, crushed

2 teaspoons Old Bay or your favorite shrimp and crab boil seasoning

2 teaspoons sugar

1/2 teaspoon whole black peppercorns

1/2 teaspoon salt

1/2 teaspoon celery salt

1/2 teaspoon celery seed

3 dried bay leaves

1 pound large shrimp (21–25 count), tails on

Cocktail Shrimp Marinade (recipe follows)

Combine all the ingredients, except the shrimp and marinade, in a large sauté pan and whisk fervently until well combined. Bring the mixture to a boil, then reduce heat and simmer for 10 minutes. Return to high heat and add the shrimp. Cook them for 2 minutes, or until they are pink and firm.

With a slotted spoon, transfer the shrimp to a colander. Reserve 1/2 cup of the cooking liquid to make a marinade for further flavoring the shrimp.

Rinse the shrimp under cool water until cooled. Peel and devein the shrimp and add to the marinade. If you'd rather not use the marinade, then dust the shrimp with Old Bay and serve with grits!

COCKTAIL SHRIMP MARINADE

1/2 cup reserved cooking liquid from the shrimp, strained

1/3 cup olive oil

1 tablespoon Dijon mustard

1/2 teaspoon minced garlic

1/2 teaspoon grated ginger or horseradish (I prefer ginger)

1 tablespoon minced onion

1 tablespoon minced celery

Juice from 1/2 lemon

1/4–1/2 cup chopped fresh parsley

1/4 cup chopped fresh chervil

Combine everything together in a large bowl and add the cooled, peeled, and deveined shrimp.

Marinate from 1 hour to overnight. The longer the shrimp marinate, the more "pickled" they become.

continued >

THE FARMER'S CLASSIC CHEESE GRITS

Grits, like other grains and starches, are not always the most flavorful elements in and of themselves, but they are a fantastic vehicle to carry other flavors throughout the dish. Grits need not always be cooked with water alone. Salt is key when it comes to cooking grits, but there's no need to add a cup of salt to boiling water just to flavor them. And don't bother salting them after they're cooked—you might as well start over.

Stock is a great way to bring flavor to grits. If I'm serving grits with seafood, then a seafood stock is an ideal cooking liquid. Chicken stock is the neutral stock of choice for cooking grits, rice, pasta and others of the sort. Just remember that with grits, it's a 1 to 4 grits-to-liquid ratio. You can make the liquid half water and half stock, all stock or even all water but with lots of aromatics and seasoning.

Cream cheese is the secret to good, creamy, luscious tasting grits. For a classic cheese grits dish to serve as the bed for shrimp, I like to use this recipe.

2 cups seafood stock

2 cups water

1 cup good-quality grits (not instant), such as those from Nora Mill

2 chicken bouillon cubes

$\frac{1}{2}$ teaspoon salt

$\frac{1}{2}$ teaspoon cracked black pepper

1 cup freshly shredded cheddar cheese (shredding your own cheese makes all the difference)

1 (8-ounce) package cream cheese

In a medium to large lidded pot, bring the liquid to a boil and add the grits, bouillon cubes, salt, and pepper. Reduce the heat and simmer for about 15 minutes, or until thickened, stirring often. Add the cheeses, stir well, and serve with shrimp on top. You can also serve these with eggs for breakfast!

BERRY PARFAIT SHOOTERS

Serves 4 to 8

Mimi always told me, "If you want it to look fancy, cut off the crust." She also said that "we eat with our eyes first." So it is only natural that the presentation of a dish—no matter how humble or simple—is especially important. Even a dish like berries with yogurt becomes fun and elegant when you pile them in a shooter-style cylindrical glass! Wake up the yogurt with a bit of honey and vanilla mixed into it, and top with roasted nuts, granola crumbles or shredded coconut.

¹⁄₄ cup honey

1 tablespoon good-quality vanilla extract

2 cups plain Greek yogurt

1 pint fresh blueberries

1 pint fresh strawberries, thinly sliced

1 pint fresh blackberries or raspberries

Mint, granola, toasted coconut or nuts, for topping

Whisk the honey and vanilla into the yogurt. In a cylindrical glass or other fun serving vessel, use the mixture as the base for your berry shooters. Top with the berries and accompaniments of your choosing.

TOMATO AND MOZZARELLA SALAD

Serves 6 to 8

Sometimes the most elegant dishes are truly the simplest. I need not explain the divine combination of tomatoes, mozzarella and vinegar, but this version is a bit of a twist on the classic threesome. Rather than just a balsamic, I use an herb-flavored vinaigrette to inject even more flavor complements to the tomatoes and mozzarella. This is an easy dressing that is great for Greek salads, summer salads and cucumber salads. It's even delish as a marinade for chicken or fish!

3/4 cup olive oil

1/2 cup red wine vinegar

1/2 teaspoon dried oregano, or 1 heaping teaspoon fresh

1/2 teaspoon dried thyme, or 1 heaping teaspoon fresh

1/2 teaspoon dried basil, or 1 heaping teaspoon fresh, chopped

3/4 teaspoon Italian seasoning

Salt and freshly ground black pepper

2 pints cherry tomatoes, halved

16 ounces mozzarella cheese, cubed or torn

In a Mason jar, combine all the dressing ingredients. Screw the lid on tightly and shake well.

Arrange the tomatoes and mozzarella on a serving platter or individual plates; drizzle the salad with the dressing. Easy and elegant!

BROCCOLI-CHEDDAR QUICHE

Makes 2 (9-inch) quiches

I love quiches. Yes, I am a man and I love quiche. I don't know where that expression of real men don't eat quiche came from, but I would like to vouch for the fact that real men who don't eat quiche are missing out. If they're not eating quiche, I'll take their share.

This particular quiche is a classic pairing of broccoli and cheddar cheese. It is a great base for adding bacon, ham or sausage, or you can make it chock-full of other veggies. For me, this simple meal appeals any time of day and is elegant enough for a luncheon or dinner party. I love that in a matter of minutes you can have this rustic yet elegant and nutritious dish full of protein and vitamins. Quiches are a building block in the culinary world—build from this block and you can add a heap of other quiches to your repertoire. I know this is cheating, but, in the interest of time and ease, using store-bought pie crusts is just fine, y'all.

---

2 store-bought pie crusts in their tin pans

Olive oil

1 small onion, diced

1 teaspoon minced garlic

1 head broccoli, trimmed and cut into florets

12 eggs

¼ cup buttermilk (or whole milk, half-and-half, or heavy cream)

Salt and freshly ground black pepper

1 heaping cup freshly shredded yellow sharp cheddar cheese

½ cup freshly shredded white cheddar cheese

Prebake the pie crusts as directed on their packaging. This will help keep your crust from being too soggy.

In a medium sauté pan, heat the oil and sauté the onion, garlic, and broccoli over medium heat until the onions are translucent and the broccoli is tender. Remove from the heat and allow to cool. (If you add these warm veggies to raw eggs, they'll scramble.)

Preheat the oven to 350 degrees F.

In a large mixing bowl, whisk the eggs and buttermilk with salt and pepper to taste until a slight froth forms at the top. Add the cooled onions and broccoli and the cheeses; gently incorporate them into the eggs.

Evenly distribute the mixture into the prebaked pie crusts and bake for 12 to 15 minutes, until the eggs are solid and the quiche does not jiggle upon moving. Serve warm or at room temperature.

MARGESON FAMILY DATE NUT CAKE

Serves 12 to 16

My friend Jess would not be a Margeson if she had not met, dated, fell in love with and married Matt. Matt and I were buddies at Auburn too, and his family hails from Albany, Georgia—not far from Perry.

The story is that Matt's Grandfather Margeson ("Gran Gran") learned this cake recipe from his Aunt Martha in Cordele; she was more of a grandmother figure to him. By helping her cut the nuts and dates, he learned how to make this cake when he was a young boy.

In Matt's lifetime, he and Gran Gran would make dozens of these cakes at the holidays for friends and family. This cake is a labor of love, and all those who the Margesons shared it with were extremely grateful.

I love this cake. It is hearty and not overly fluffy or too sweet. It's almost, dare I say, like a fruitcake! I love it with whipped cream! I am so thankful to the Margesons for sharing this cake with me. I love the story that accompanies the recipe, for it is often through our recipes that we learn our history and heritage—and through those recipes is how we continue the feast!

---

1 cup all-purpose flour

2 teaspoons baking powder

1/4 teaspoon salt

4 cups pecans—cut, not chopped

1 pound dates, chopped

1 cup sugar

4 eggs, separated

2 teaspoons vanilla extract

Preheat the oven to 250 degrees F with a shallow pan of water on the top rack. Leave the pan of water in the oven for the first 30 minutes of baking time.

Mix together the flour, baking powder, salt, nuts, and dates thoroughly and allow the mixture to set for 1 hour.

Cream together the sugar and egg yolks, and add the vanilla. Mix with the flour mixture.

Beat the egg whites until frothy, then fold them into the egg, sugar, and flour mixture.

Line a tube pan with greased waxed paper. (I like to grease both sides of the waxed paper with spray oil then line the tube.) Pour the batter into the lined pan.

Bake for 1 hour and 20 minutes, or until a toothpick comes out clean from the center. Remove from the oven and allow to cool on a wire rack for about 30 minutes.

MAMA JUNE'S CARROT CAKE

Serves 12 to 16

Mama June is a nurse by trade, so she has always had to doctor us up—body and soul—from our childhood onward. She can make a mighty good carrot cake, which I think is a part of being a healing individual, for sometimes what we really need to make us better is a good carrot cake.

We have talked about this carrot cake recipe and others too. The common denominator is that often a carrot cake is a tad dry. Even though the carrots themselves are mainly water, many carrot cakes still come out dry. The secret to Mama June's, she told me, was the not completely drained can of crushed pineapple. And I love how Mama June dictated the recipe to me as if I were her hospital orderly. To-the-point baking—I like that!

Mrs. June and Mr. Doug—a history professor and country music songwriter extraordinaire—have always been so encouraging to me and my friends, and they gave Jess her hard-working sensibility, knack for learning, knowledge of history and drive to succeed. They often are amazed by right-brained creative types such as Jess and me, and we are amazed at them since they can do math!

I am so grateful to many of my friends' parents, who made me their friend too—especially when they have shared their recipe cards! Thank you, Mama June!

---

2 cups all-purpose flour

2 teaspoons baking soda

1/2 teaspoon salt

2 teaspoons cinnamon

3 eggs, well beaten

3/4 cups vegetable oil

3/4 cup buttermilk

2 cups sugar

2 teaspoons vanilla extract

2 cups grated carrots

1 (8-ounce) can crushed pineapple, mostly drained

1 (3.5-ounce) can (1 1/3 cups) flaked, sweetened coconut

1 cup chopped pecans or walnuts

Cream Cheese Frosting (recipe follows)

Preheat the oven to 350 degrees F. Grease and lightly flour two 9-inch round cake pans; set aside.

Sift or whisk the flour, baking soda, salt, and cinnamon until well blended. Set aside.

Combine the eggs, oil, buttermilk, sugar, and vanilla. Beat until smooth.

Stir flour mixture into the egg and oil mixture; blend well. Stir in the carrots, pineapple, coconut, and nuts.

Pour the batter into the prepared pans. Bake for 35 to 40 minutes, or until a toothpick inserted into the center of the cake comes out clean.

Allow the cake to cool in the pan for at least 15 minutes. Remove from the pan, cool completely, then ice with the frosting.

CREAM CHEESE FROSTING

Makes about 3 cups

1 (8-ounce) package cream cheese, softened

1/2 cup (1 stick) butter, softened

1 (1-pound) box confectioners' sugar

1 teaspoon vanilla extract

Use a mixer to combine all the ingredients until well blended and smooth.

Refrigerate if not serving immediately.

Baby Henry and Baby Evelyn's First Birthdays

First birthdays are chock-full of fun! When else does a child get to eat as much cake as he or she can handle while wearing only a diaper? They can smash the cake, clasp it with their tiny fists, stuff it in their mouths and even wipe sugary icing on their faces—and on the faces of their parents too—! (I'm sure we could do this at our older birthdays, but we would probably lack an adoring audience beaming with pride and encouraging us to fill our cheeks with icing!)

Two babies in my life have had their special first birthdays, and we celebrated them in true Southern style. My best friend Maggie Coody Griffin hosted her Henry's first birthday at her parents' home in Hawkinsville. First birthdays with this family and mine go back many years. In fact, when Mama was planning my baby sister Meredith's first birthday, Mrs. Joni Coody casually offered to help if she could. Mama's reply to her darling friend Joni's cordial offer was, "Yes, Joni! You're so sweet for asking . . . do you mind churning the ice cream?" This was to be no easy task, y'all. "No good deed goes unpunished" is a mantra I have come to believe in.

You see, Meredith's party turned into a soirée, for this one-year-old's party was held under a yellow-and-white-striped tent on the lawn of an old antebellum home in Hawkinsville. In the heat of a Southern July, Mrs. Joni churned enough ice cream for nearly a hundred folks—and enough for them to come back for

seconds! Thankfully, she had her precious mother-in-law's recipe; Mama Doris knew how to feed a crowd! To this day, Mrs. Joni swears that the sound of an ice cream churn takes her back to Meredith's party and maybe even the start of her labor with her baby Asa! Ha!

Jesse Noble is the lead designer in my interior design firm. Though the company is officially James Farmer Designs, the ladies in my office run the show! I'm a smart man, for I hire smarter women! I hardly know anyone else with such a determined work ethic, flawless style and polite business demeanor. Plus, Jesse has the kindest, gentlest spirit that shines through to every person she encounters. And it doesn't hurt that her baby girls, Charlotte and Evelyn, are absolutely adorable!

Jesse and Roy hosted Baby Evelyn's first birthday at their home. We Southerners love a reason to "fluff" our houses and celebrate with friends and family in our own nests! Jesse, being an interior designer and tremendously thoughtful soul, evokes both comfort and style in her home. I cannot thank her enough for marrying a local boy, moving down to "Perrydise" from Atlanta and working with me! Or do I work for Jesse? Let's just say that I say "yes, ma'am" most of the day in my office.

Jesse and I have the privilege of working in and designing homes for our clients across the South. So

MENU

Joni's Pimento
Cheese Sandwiches

Mommy's Black Bean Dip

Pammy's Pound Cake

Mama Doris's Peach
Ice Cream

The Coody's Ice
Cream "Casserole"

Iced Sugar Cookies

Fruit Kabobs with
Caramel Sauce

PB&J Hearts

Wilson's Petit Fours

Raspberry Agua Freeze

when we are able to entertain folks at our homes, the cause for celebration is truly close to our hearts—baby Evelyn's first birthday included! When else is there a better time to celebrate with pink icing and flowers, pink plaid and balloons, a pink drink, and even pink plates, cups, and napkins?! And don't forget a pink crown too! This little princess was truly "pretty in pink" for her special day!

Evie and big sister Charlotte are close in age, as are many other sibling sets in our town. This works great for parties in Perry—the more the merrier! When celebrating the lives of these children—the children of my childhood friends and contemporaries too—I cannot help but be filled with joy! Many of these babies call me "Uncle Jay," and I am thrilled and honored to have such a role in their lives. The treasures these children's lives bring into mine are countless and abounding. Plus, these are the children who will watch us eat birthday cake in our diapers when we have grown old! Ha! Happy first birthday, Henry and Evie!

JONI'S PIMENTO CHEESE SANDWICHES

Serves a gracious plenty

In the South, whether it is your first or last birthday party, you will have pimento cheese. Mrs. Joni Coody's recipe has been a staple for feeding her brood, as well as ours, for as long as I can remember! Every well-bred Southern lady knows that cutting the crust off the bread makes it "fancy." Little rounds and squares of de-crusted pimento cheese sandwiches are expected at just about any Southern affair. Baboo (Mrs. Joni's mama) and Mimi (my mama's mama) taught us all so much about entertaining graciously and loving wholeheartedly—even if a pimento cheese sandwich is all you're serving.

What I love about Mrs. Joni's Pimento Cheese is that it's a classic recipe, well suited for any occasion, but with a peppery twist. Mrs. Joni herself can be described as a classic that's well suited for any occasion! She can't help it, I'm afraid—she was raised right!

For a more rustic spread, you can mix or blend the cheeses by hand. For a smoother spread, use a food processor.

---

2 (8-ounce) blocks sharp cheddar cheese, shredded

1 (8-ounce) block mild white cheddar cheese, shredded

1 (8-ounce) block cream cheese, softened

2 (7-ounce) jars pimentos, drained

1/2–3/4 cup pickled jalapeño slices, drained and roughly chopped (depending on your heat tolerance)

1 (12-ounce) jar roasted red bell peppers, drained and roughly chopped

1/2 cup mayonnaise (more or less to get your desired creaminess)

2 tablespoons Worcestershire sauce

Dash of garlic powder

Dash of 5th Season seasoned salt

Salt and freshly ground black pepper

1 loaf bread

Combine the cheeses using a food processor, then add all the other ingredients. Mix everything until well combined. Spread on half of your bread slices and top the sandwiches with the other half. Cut off crusts, cut sandwiches diagonally or into rounds and serve.

FARMER'S NOTE: *This recipe is meant for a crowd. You can cut it in half if you're not feeding the whole herd. But pimento cheese will keep for a week in the refrigerator and it is a great gift to take to a party or neighbor. This version also makes a great "cheese ball" and is so good on crackers with jam or jelly too.*

MOMMY'S BLACK BEAN DIP

Serves 12 or more

My sisters have called me "Brubbs" since childhood. Southern familial nicknames and their longevity throughout one's life are legendary. You may be christened one name and called something completely different by your family and friends. I am James Theodore Farmer III, and I'm actually the first to be called "James." My grandfather Farmer, Daddy Ted, went by Ted, but "Henry" more often. "Henry" he was called by his brothers, and it stuck. A lady told me one time that she knew "Henry Farmer" growing up and asked, "Where did the 'James' come from?" I had to inform her that James is our Christian name.

So, nicknames live long in the South. And when my friends became parents, parental names were added to their list of Christian and proper and nicknames too. When Thomas Henry Griffin was born, Maggie and David became Mommy and Daddy. And so titles this dip—Mommy's Black Bean Dip. Whether you call her Maggie or Mommy, I'm sure y'all will love this dip as much as we do! It has become a staple for parties and appetizers in our circle.

I love this for topping burgers or grilled chicken too. You can serve it over greens as a salad; it is a perfect bed for a filet of fish, or is ideal whipped and pureed as a hummus-style dip or spread! Y'all enjoy!

---

2 (15-ounce) cans black beans (I use the reduced sodium)

1 red bell pepper, chopped

1 yellow bell pepper, chopped

1 orange bell pepper, chopped

1 green bell pepper, chopped

1/2 medium red onion, chopped

2 ripe mangoes, peeled and chopped

2 teaspoons freshly chopped cilantro

2 scallions, chopped

1/2 medium jalapeño, chopped (don't forget your gloves!)

3 tablespoons olive oil

Juice of 2 limes

1 teaspoon kosher salt

1 (15-ounce) can fiesta corn

Handful of grape tomatoes, chopped

1 avocado, peeled and chopped

Tortilla chips, for serving

Combine all the ingredients, let chill for 1 hour, and serve with your favorite snack chips!

PAMMY'S POUND CAKE

Serves 12 to 16

Mrs. Pam Griffin is Henry Griffin's paternal grandmother. Her son, David, and I grew up together, and I count him as a most trusted, dependable and even-keeled friend. This, of course, is a true testament to David's character and good raising!

"Pammy" became Mrs. Pam's nickname when her first grandchild came along. As true Southern children, we are all taught that ladies—especially teachers—are always called and referred to as "Miss" and their last name. If the lady is a teacher but also the mama of your good buddy David, then you can run into some confusion as to addressing her—she's a teacher and a friend's mama!

You see, Southern children refer to their friend's mothers as "Mrs." and her first name. If she does happen to be a teacher and a friend's mama, then she graciously tells you to call her "Mrs. Pam." But when grandbabies come along, Pammy and other grandmother nomenclature becomes de rigueur and acceptable. This is further evidence that grandchildren can do no wrong in their grandparents' eyes—especially when they can break down the Southern code for proper names!

Pammy's Pound Cake is a Griffin-family classic. Fresh from the oven, sliced and served with whipped cream and fruit, or toasted the next day, a pound cake is the Southern cornerstone for desserts. Every family has their version, and I'm thankful that Miss Griffin—aka Mrs. Pam or Pammy—shares hers with us! Her recipe comes from her grandmother, which makes it that much more special! We Southerners pass on names and recipes along with our genes!

---

2 sticks butter, softened (aged if possible)

2 cups sugar

2 cups all-purpose flour

5 eggs

Beat the butter and sugar together until fluffy. Add the flour and 1 egg at a time alternately, beginning and ending with flour.

Add the batter to a lightly greased and floured Bundt pan. Pammy's grandmother's note on the recipe says, "Do not wash it," for many of these old-fashioned, heavier pans would keep the "seasoning" from previous cakes. I always grease and flour the pan for security.

Start in a cold oven and bake at 325 degrees F for about 1 hour, or until a toothpick comes out clean. I always start checking at 50 minutes. Just don't stomp around the kitchen or slam the oven door!

MAMA DORIS'S PEACH ICE CREAM

Makes 1 gallon plus

The Coody children and the Farmer children received one of the greatest gifts a child can ever receive—they both had devoted, graceful, elegant, loving, supporting Southern grandmothers. Mama Doris made the best peach ice cream. Churning homemade peach ice cream on a screened-in back porch on a warm summer evening, with the scent of jasmine and honeysuckle lightly perfuming the humid air, is a memory millions of Southerners share—secondary only to the memories of our beloved grandmothers.

    Peach ice cream is a reward. Picking and peeling peaches is no easy task, and waiting with childlike enthusiasm for the ice cream to chill and churn can be as slow as molasses in January—slow for us grown-up children too! For me, peach ice cream is a slice of summer's freshest jewels that I will always associate fondly with beach trips, birthday parties, Fourth of July at the lake, and time with my closest friends and family. Not many dishes can call up so many fond memories as does peach ice cream. And when the recipe is from a lady as fine as Mama Doris was, it makes the dish even more of a treasure.

---

2 quarts fresh peaches, chopped in a food processor or blender

2 tablespoons vanilla extract

1 teaspoon salt

2 (14-ounce) cans sweetened condensed milk

1 (13-ounce) can evaporated milk

½ cup sugar (none if the peaches are already sweet, or adjust the amount to your liking)

½ gallon whole milk

Ice

Rock salt

    To the inner canister of a 6-quart ice cream churn, add the peaches, vanilla, salt, condensed milk, evaporated milk, and sugar. Stir together.

    Fill the canister to the "fill" line with the milk. Close the lid, pack the ice and rock salt around the inner canister, and churn until ice cream is ready.

FARMER'S NOTE: For a bit of tangy goodness, try replacing some of the whole milk with 1 cup buttermilk. I love how the buttermilk tones down the sweetness and give a zip too!

THE COODYS' ICE CREAM "CASSEROLE"

Makes a 9 x 13-inch pan

Mrs. Susie raised the Coody children. Her best friend, Mrs. Mary, has raised the Farmer children and fed us with Southern soul and comfort food for generations. There is a wonderful rivalry between the two ladies as to who has the better biscuits, fried chicken or squash casserole. Let's just say the two families might even egg the rivalry on in order for another pan of biscuits to competitively appear.

One time as children, we had dinner at the Coody house. Maggie Farmer (we have to say Maggie Farmer and Maggie Coody to keep our stories somewhat straight), Meredith and I came home and raved about Mrs. Joni's Ice Cream Casserole! Mama had to get the recipe from Mrs. Joni; if not, her children may never have eaten again due to the hunger strike we swore would ensue. Since then, I am ashamed of how many times I have devoured this "casserole," whether made by Jeanie or Joni. Mama swore that Joni's was better. "It is like a sandwich—if someone else makes it, it just tastes better," Mama always said. I often encouraged both ladies to make an Ice Cream Casserole and let me be the judge.

In the South, there are customary funeral foods. Different denominations bring different dishes: Baptists bring casseroles, Methodists and Presbyterians typically bring a "meat and three" meal, and Episcopalians bring liquor. Towns can differ as to whether fried chicken or a pound cake is the first dish that is proper to bring the bereaved. Regardless, both dishes will appear—and in large quantities, I assure you. After the wake or a week or so of feeding the grieving family passes, the barrage of fried chicken and pound cake subsides, and the shock of real life without mounds of funeral food begins to set in. It is here that dearest friends step in, call you to come to supper, take you to dinner or make you a favorite childhood dessert—Ice Cream Casserole.

Though not a "casserole" proper, this dessert is made in a 9 x 13-inch glass dish, which to any Southerner is a casserole dish. We may not all be Baptists, but we have all had our share of casseroles—ice cream or otherwise. Y'all enjoy!

---

1 1/2 cups crushed crunchy peanut butter cereal

1/3 cup firmly packed dark brown sugar

1/3 cup melted butter

1/2 cup chopped nuts (such as walnuts or pecans, but salted peanuts are good too)

1/2 gallon chocolate or vanilla ice cream, softened

1/3 cup butter, room temperature

1 cup powdered sugar

2 egg yolks

1 square unsweetened chocolate, melted and cooled

1/4-1/2 gallon chocolate or vanilla ice cream, softened

Combine the cereal, brown sugar, melted butter, and chopped nuts. Mash half of the mixture into the bottom of a 9 x 13-inch baking dish.

Cover the mixture with 1/2 gallon of your favorite chocolate or vanilla ice cream. (I like to use chocolate for this layer.)

Beat the butter and powdered sugar until creamy, and then blend in the egg yolks.

Add the chocolate to the butter, sugar, and egg yolk mixture. Spread this on top of the first ice cream layer. Place in the freezer to harden or set.

Spread 1/4 to 1/2 gallon ice cream (I like vanilla at this stage) atop the chocolate layer. Cover with the other half of the cereal mixture. Keep frozen until ready to serve.

ICED SUGAR COOKIES

Makes a medium-size batch of cookies

Simple, elegant and flavored just right, the sugar cookie is the cornerstone of the cookie kingdom! Whether akin to shortbread or slightly chewy, covered in icing or sprinkles, or flavored with vanilla, almond or lemon, sugar cookies are a classic part of Southern celebrations and holidays.

Every town has a cookie lady, a pound cake baker or that little lady in the church that makes and sells the best caramel cakes. Each generation has to have someone to take the torch and continue the tradition. I love that my generation has someone keeping the art of sugar cookies alive and well. I could hardly bear the thought of a birthday, wedding or holiday without an iced sugar cookie, festively decorated and depicting the event's theme!

Lucky for us, our friend Linsey McCord Freeman is carrying on the sugar cookie tradition in our town. Linsey joins the ranks of good ol' Southern ladies that make our parties wonderful events with their festive food. From giraffes to monogrammed rattles, Linsey has made sugar cookies in all shapes in sizes.

This is my easy version of iced sugar cookies. I hope y'all roll out some fun for your family and friends and even get the kids involved! Cookie making at the holidays is one of my fondest memories.

---

2 sticks butter, room temperature

$^2/_3$ cup sugar

1 egg

1 $^1/_2$ teaspoons vanilla extract

1 teaspoon almond extract* (optional)

2 $^1/_2$ cups sifted all-purpose flour

$^1/_2$ teaspoon salt

FOR THE ICING:

1 $^1/_2$ cups powdered sugar

1 tablespoon milk

$^1/_2$ teaspoon or more almond extract (optional)

Food coloring and other cookie decorations to your liking

Cream together the butter and sugar, then beat in the egg, vanilla extract, and almond extract.

In a separate bowl, combine the flour and salt, then stir it into the butter-and-sugar mixture. Cover the dough with plastic wrap and chill for 30 minutes to 1 hour, until firm.

Preheat the oven to 350 degrees F, and grease a cookie sheet or line with parchment paper.

On a lightly floured surface or board, roll out the chilled dough to desired thickness. I like a thicker cookie, but a thinner ($^1/_4$-inch) cookie is a great thickness and not too puffy. Cut out with cookie cutters of your choosing, or simply cut into rounds.

Place the cookies on the cookie sheet and bake for 8 to 9 minutes. I like to take them out just as the edges are turning brown. Transfer the cookies to a wire rack to cool completely while you're making the icing.

For the icing, sift the powdered sugar into a bowl and add the milk and almond extract. Stir until smooth. You may need another splash of milk (about 1 teaspoon). Divide and dye the icing to your desired color. Ice cookies with a knife or pipe on with cake decorating tools. Add decorations of your preference.

*You can substitute lemon for a citrusy spine. If you prefer vanilla extract only, use a total of 3 teaspoons for the recipe.

FRUIT KABOBS WITH CARAMEL SAUCE

Grown-ups and kiddos alike all have to eat at a child's party, and fruit seems to be the bridge between more mature palates and younger taste buds. Fruit kabobs are limited only by your imagination and creativity for combining fruit on a skewer, but I do love the combination of apples and caramel!

To the skewered apples, I like to add some creaminess with brie. Brie and fruit are classic flavors, and the caramel sauce is simply an added bonus. Tart green apples, sweet red apples, creamy brie and a drizzle of caramel will make any child or grown-up happy! The sweet-and-tart flavor of dried cranberries is a fun touch too. And who doesn't love a bit of salt with their sweet? Small flaked sea salt is perfect!

Apples or other fruit of your choice

Brie, sliced into wedges

Dried cranberries

Caramel Sauce (recipe follows)

Sea salt flakes (optional)

Slice apples or other fruit and skewer them onto bamboo skewers, alternating with wedges of brie. Sprinkle dried cranberries for garnish and drizzle with caramel sauce. Sprinkle lightly with sea salt if you desire.

CARAMEL SAUCE

Makes about 5 cups

3 cups sugar

1 cup (2 sticks) butter

1 ½ cups milk

Here's the key—constant stirring! Cook the sugar and butter together over high heat, stirring constantly, until the mixture turns amber color. Remove from the heat and allow the mixture to cool slowly. Add the milk slowly and reheat until slightly warm, beating until smooth.

HAPPY
BIRTHDAY

Evelyn Kate
is turning ONE

Please join us for
her special celebration
Sunday
January 11th at 3 o'clock

204 Idle Pines Drive
Perry, GA 31069

*a little cake,
a lot of fun,
Henry is turning ONE!*

PB&J HEARTS

Serves as many as you want

Who doesn't "heart" PB&J? Especially if the sandwich is in the shape of a heart? Though making a PB&J doesn't require master chef credentials, there a few ideas I feel are important to remember in making the best ones, giving tradition a twist!

Mixing the ingredients: I love to mix the peanut butter and jelly before spreading the bread. Peanut butter and jelly are perhaps a child's first experiment with sweet and salty combos, and there's something so delicious about the two when mixed just right. If you care for it to be a tad sweeter, use more jelly. If you care for it to be a tad saltier, use more peanut butter.

Honey, don't forget the honey: Honey, like jelly, adds sweetness, but a different flavor. I love to use it with both peanut butter and jelly or with peanut butter alone.

Fruit and fruit preserves: Fig and strawberry preserves are luscious with salty peanut butter. Their sweet chewiness and the crunchy saltiness of peanut butter are delicious together. Thinly sliced Granny Smith apples are amazing additions to a PB&J too. That tart crispness adds a lovely element. Bananas, pears and sliced strawberries all are fun on a classic PB&J!

Toasted PB&Js: Day-old biscuits and cornbread, pound cake, homemade bread—so many things are almost better the next day when lightly buttered and toasted. Try toasting your PB&J in a lightly buttered or greased skillet, just to warm everything through and make it all delightfully gooey!

PB and? Out of jelly? Or care to explore some other combos? Try peanut butter mixed with Nutella, marshmallow cream, a thin layer of cream cheese or even apple butter. These are further ways to expound upon the wonders of sweet and salty that are ever so delectable on soft white or wheat bread—no matter which birthday you're having this year!

WILSON'S PETIT FOURS

Makes 16

Wilson's Bakery in Warner Robins has been baking and selling goodies for over sixty years. I am one of three generations of my family who have come to rely on them for every season, event and celebration: jack-o'-lantern cookies at Halloween, Easter confections, ladyfingers with a stripe of colored icing nodding to the season, Christmas treats, and birthday cakes piled high with piped icing, confectionery charms and designs aplenty for any child's taste. In our county, you don't turn 1 or 100 without a Wilson's cake!

For Baby Evie's first birthday, a Wilson's confectionery creation was in store for this real-life baby doll! The yellow cake was simply delicious, layered in swirly shades of pink icing and topped with a "bow." Though I could eat an entire birthday cake if I set my mind to it, I probably shouldn't. Yet I can devour as many petit fours as I can handle, because they're really just bites of cakey goodness—no real calories of any merit, right? Ha!

As Southerners, we will monogram anything that sits still, and petit fours are no exception. To make the sugary, glazed cake squares truly Southern, Evelyn Kate's "EK" initials were piped onto Wilson's petit fours in rosy pink and trimmed with lime green. They were the perfect addition to Evie's first birthday party!

Here is my take on a classic petit four. I hope I make Wilson's proud!

1/4 cup butter, room temperature

1/4 cup shortening

1 cup sugar

1 teaspoon good-quality vanilla extract

1 1/3 cups all-purpose flour

2 teaspoons baking powder

1/2 teaspoon salt

2/3 cup buttermilk plus 1 tablespoon milk

3 egg whites

FOR THE GLAZE:

2 pounds powdered sugar

2/3 cup water

1 tablespoon good-quality vanilla extract

1 tablespoon almond extract

Grease a 9-inch-square metal baking pan, and preheat the oven to 350 degrees F.

In a large bowl, cream together the butter, shortening, and sugar until light and fluffy. Beat in the vanilla by hand. Sift the flour and combine with the baking powder and salt. Alternating with the buttermilk, add the flour mixture to the creamed mixture in thirds, beginning and ending with flour; beat well after each addition.

In a small bowl, beat the egg whites until soft peaks form, then gently fold into the batter.

Pour the batter into the prepared baking pan. Bake for 20 to 25 minutes, or until a toothpick inserted near the center comes out clean. Allow the cake to cool for 10 minutes before removing from the pan to a wire rack or counter to cool completely.

Here's where cake turns into petit fours! Remove the cake from the pan and cut a thin slice off each side of the cake, making it as square as possible. Cut the cake into about 1 1/4-inch squares. Line them up about 1/2 inch apart on a rack set in a large baking pan or sheet.

For the glaze, combine all the ingredients and mix on low speed just until blended. Then beat on high until smooth and creamy. If the mixture is too thick, add up to 2 tablespoons water to thin it. Using a mixing spoon, pour the glaze atop each cake square, allowing the excess to drizzle down the sides. Allow the glaze to cool and harden slightly.

COLORED FROSTING

6 tablespoons softened butter

2 tablespoons shortening

1 tablespoon vanilla extract (or substitute another extract or your choosing)

3 cups powdered sugar

4 tablespoons milk

Food coloring of choice

If you want to frost the petit fours or decorate them using cake decorating tips, cream the butter, shortening and vanilla in a small bowl. Beat in the powdered sugar and just enough milk to achieve the desired consistency. Place about $\frac{1}{2}$ to $\frac{3}{4}$ cup frosting into each of two bowls. Tint one icing pink and one green, or use colors of your choice.

RASPBERRY AGUA FRESCA

Serves 8

Refreshing water or "fresh cold water"—just the name of this classic drink in English or Spanish is delightful. It is basically taking plain water and adding some fruit for a medley of refreshment. Easily made for a crowd or just a couple of folks, this beverage lends itself to interpretation, based on taste and the season.

Often made with melons, pineapple or tropical fruit, agua fresca can be served in a myriad of ways. Cantaloupe, watermelon, and honeydew make this drink a gorgeous color. I also like to mix pineapple and strawberries for a luscious, colorful batch, but for Evie's party, raspberries matched our color scheme! Fun glass jars and containers make perfect vessels to dish out this drink. Their rippled, wavy composition is a fun alternative to a plain glass pitcher. This recipe is easily reduced or doubled, so you can ladle up glass after glass of this refreshment for your own porch or party!

10 heaping cups fruit (such as melon, raspberries, other berries, and/or pineapple)

1 cup simple syrup of your choice*

1/2 cup freshly squeezed lemon juice

1/2 cup freshly squeezed lime juice

8 cups water

10 pounds ice cubes

Fruit, for garnish (raspberries, or use the same kind of fruit in your agua fresca for your garnish.)

In a food processor or blender, puree your fruit of choice. Be sure to scrape down the sides to get all the goodness! Add the simple syrup, lemon juice, and lime juice and puree again until smooth.

Pour the fruit puree into a large serving vessel, then add the water and ice to your desired consistency. Mix well and ladle up! Add some whole raspberries to float in the water too!

*Plain simple syrup is just fine; that's equal parts sugar and water heated together until the sugar has dissolved. But an herbal one gives a nice kick! We used my mint simple syrup for Evie's party; just infuse the syrup with some garden mint while you're heating it, then remove the herbs.

Retirement Celebration for Virginia Monroe

Just before her retirement, the Reverend Virginia Monroe was the priest at Church of the Good Shepherd in Cashiers, North Carolina. It is safe to say that everyone in her parish, along with all those that know her in general, consider her not only their priest proper but also their confidant, shoulder to cry on, sage advisor, counselor, keeper of the faith and simply dearest friend in life's simplest and grandest of times. I could say more about her and will stand in line with many, many other folks who concur.

There has been a season of loss in my life, of not only my grandmother but my mother as well—both within a year's time. What I find so amazing is how friends and family unite together and reform the brokenness and disconnection you feel. Through these losses—ones that are never completely recoverable—we become banded through the bonds of friends gathering together and familial ties strengthening, thus drawing us closer in ways that we never expected.

Cashiers is my happy place and has been since childhood. I am not shy about my love for the mountains there—the grandeur of the natural majesty and the awesome humility you feel surrounded by the granite faces of Whiteside and the other surrounding crests, peaks, ridges and forest. When I'm in Cashiers on a summer Sunday, I love to attend Summer Chapel—a little white schoolhouse turned Sunday chapel. There

in the valley between Cashiers and Highlands, overlooking the splendorous collision of mountain and meadow, the banjo-led musicians lead the congregation in old-timey hymns and spirituals. A brief homily and communion brings the congregation together, and friends join one another for lunch afterwards.

There at Summer Chapel one Sunday morning, Virginia Monroe was the guest preacher. Though I knew her socially through dear mutual friends, I had not heard her preach. From her cadence to a story about an apple cake and even her curly hair, I immediately felt as if my Mimi were speaking directly to me from that very pulpit. I was given a sense of peace that surpasses worldly understanding—a peace only divinely given. I knew that the wellspring of love instilled in me by my mother and grandmother was not dry. It was there, waiting to be tapped once again—and once again ready to be poured forth on others from the depth of grace, love, joy and zeal for life, just as it did from Mama's and Mimi's wellsprings.

Virginia will always say that she was just the messenger that Sunday morning, but I tell her over and over that while that may be true, it doesn't stop me from telling her that Mimi was preaching to me that day! Virginia became my Mountain Mimi, and we have shared some exceptional fun together with our friends over the past couple of years.

MENU

Herb-Rolled Goat Cheese

Smoked Trout Dip

Lucky Money

Lynwood's Pasta Salad

Fluffy Ambrosia

Mile-High Cornbread

Mashed Sweet Potatoes

Roasted Pork Tenderloin with
Bourbon Mustard Sauce

Sweet-and-Sour
Braised Red Cabbage

Goat Cheese Cheesecake with
Sour Cream Caramel Sauce

Julie's Spiced Carrot Cake

Though none of us were ready for her to retire, it was her time. I felt it the utmost honor and privilege when, the summer before her retirement, she confided to me and our close friend Cindy Moore that she would be retiring that coming January. Then she said that she thought it would be a simple occasion—coffee and cake in the parish hall after her sermon, with maybe fifty or so attendees.

Cindy and I noticed a sense of worry on Virginia's never-worried face, and when we asked her "what about the other 200 people that will be there?" Virginia's humility would not allow her think there would be any great number of folks in Cashiers on a cold January morning just to wish her their best after thirteen years at Good Shepherd.

Cindy, who is like another mother to me, and I often think on the same wavelength and immediately knew *we* had to plan the party—a little cake and a pot of coffee would not do! I told Virginia to leave the party to us and to focus on her sermon. The menu immediately came to mind since it was near New Year's, and if the task to feed a couple hundred folks in the mountains was at hand, I needed Chef Jason Whitaker, the Frou Frou floral crew and the hostess committee at the church too! Cindy gave me some of the best party and entertaining advice with true maternal wisdom. She said, "Always hire the best caterer. That is the extent of my culinary contribution to you, son."

We decked the hall, literally, in fresh-cut Fraser firs from a parishioner's tree farm, festooned all the tables in kelly green checkered linens and stacked enough blue splatterware to help us truly "keep the feast" going! I didn't want to just keep the feast—I wanted the feast to continue ad infinitum! That became our theme as the planning came down to execution and the day drew close! Virginia kept the feast as rector at Good Shepherd, and I know she'll continue her feast with her legacy and continued ministry, though not as a robed minister.

The Southern New Year's menu is a wealth of hope for health, luck, good fortune and moving forward in life. Black-eyed peas, collard greens, cornbread, pork tenderloins, ambrosia and desserts to sweeten the day filled out the menu and fed us well into the afternoon. White amaryllis, quince blossoms, magnolia, orchids, roses in shades of cream, white, ivory and chartreuse all kept the fresh start in mind with their palette. From food to flowers, the celebration feast and the season of gratitude were all held close and appealed to the senses. A feast kept and a feast continued—celebration of a tenure and heritage and love for my sweet friend and our priest, The Reverend Virginia Monroe.

It is through grief that *joy* is made sweeter and through friends that family is restored—I can testify to that truth!

HERB-ROLLED GOAT CHEESE

This is a simple starter to spread on crackers, toast, pita chips or crudités. It looks great on a platter by itself or on a cheese board.

I have been a fan of block cream cheese with pepper jelly oozing down its sides as my appetizer of choice for as long as I can remember—until I tried it with a log of goat cheese. Then I started exploring other ways to ensure that logs of goat cheese could infiltrate my entertaining and repertoire. Who doesn't try to inject their daily life with goat cheese?

Cream cheese and pepper jelly is still an all-time fave—my friend Lauri Jo's Pineapple Pepper jelly is my favorite. I always know what I'm getting for Christmas and keep a jar of her pepper jelly on reserve to pull out when impromptu dinner parties arise or I just want a snack! Try the Pineapple Pepper Jelly with a log of goat cheese—mmmm-mmmm!

1/8 cup minced rosemary

1/8 cup minced parsley

1 tablespoon dried pepper flakes

1 teaspoon dried minced onion

Heavy dash of garlic salt

Dash of lemon pepper

1/2 teaspoon cracked black pepper

Coarse sea salt

1 log of goat cheese of available size

Mix the herbs and seasoning together and sprinkle them on a cutting board or work surface. Roll the log of goat cheese in the herbs and seasoning and arrange on a platter or cheese tray.

FARMER'S NOTE ON CHEESE BOARDS AND CHEESE STRAWS: Cheese boards are terrific for entertaining. Remember to pair complementary flavors with one another, such as Parmesan with pears, green apples with brie, sharp cheddar with crisp and sweet apples and strawberries with blue cheese. And, of course, cheese straws go great with anything!

SMOKED TROUT DIP

Serves 8 or more

This dip is one we all clamor for when we're together in the mountains. From the streams, rivers and lakes, trout are caught and then smoked and used to make this hearty dip for cocktail time on the porch and in the best restaurants too. I love to take some crème fraîche to tame the smoky fish and flavor it further with shallot and dill.

Some of my favorite times in the mountains are sitting on the porch with friends, eating appetizers for dinner as the sun sets behind the Whiteside and Devil's Courthouse. Laughter and storytelling ensue and the nights are cool—a luxury for wilted Southerners in summertime. I love to mix crispy toasted crackers with raw and pickled veggies as vehicles for the dip.

2 smoked trout fillets (about 8 ounces total), skinned and boned

1 small shallot, chopped

⅓ cup crème fraîche or sour cream

½ cup heavy cream

2 tablespoons chopped fresh dill

1 teaspoon freshly ground black pepper

A tiny bit of fresh lemon juice

In a food processor, pulse trout, shallot, crème fraîche, and cream together until smooth. Add dill and pepper, then pulse just to combine. Serve with crackers and a tiny squeeze of fresh lemon juice.

LUCKY MONEY

Serves 8 or more

For the New Year's Day menu, Southerners eat a set menu, with some interpretation but predominately the same meal across the South. Black-eyed peas are eaten for luck and collard greens (or greens in general) are eaten for money. Combine the two, and you have Lucky Money!

I love to make a Lucky Money stew, for the greens and peas are so succulent when cooked together with ham hock and with some added heat from a few jalapeños. As legend has it, destitute and Civil War–distraught and starving Southerners began to eat the fodder that was to feed the cattle in order to survive. The fodder was known as cowpeas, naturally, and they became known for their hallmark black "eyes."

Black-eyed peas helped many folks survive, luckily, and thus the tradition of black-eyed peas bringing luck was born in the South.

¼ cup olive oil

2 tablespoons minced garlic

5 cups chicken stock

1 ham hock or ½ pound country ham

5 bunches collard greens, rinsed, trimmed, and chopped

2 cups dried black-eyed peas

Salt and black pepper

4 small jalapeños, chopped

Heat olive oil in a large pot over medium heat. Add garlic, and gently sauté until light brown. Pour in the chicken stock and add the ham. Cover the pot and simmer for 30 minutes.

Add the collard greens and peas to the cooking pot, and turn the heat up to medium-high. Let the greens and peas cook down for about 45 minutes, stirring occasionally. The peas should be tender but not mushy.

Reduce heat to medium, and season with salt and pepper to taste. Continue to cook until the greens are tender and dark green, 45 to 60 minutes. Drain greens, reserving the liquid. Mix in jalapeños if desired. Use the reserved liquid or chicken stock to reheat leftovers.

LYNWOOD'S PASTA SALAD

Serves 4 to 6

Lynwood Hall is an acclaimed artist, fabulous cook, and "host with the most" known for his parties. Thankfully, he is one of my dearest friends.

Hailing from Moultrie, Georgia, Lynwood and I share a roster of mutual friends from Savannah to Atlanta and every small town in between. We both serve on the State Botanical Board for Georgia and are quite dangerous when our powers are combined at a dinner party. Much of our time is spent in Cashiers rather than South Georgia, for Cashiers is invaded by citizens of the Deep South once summer's heat is in full swing. Porch parties in Cashiers become our soirées, where the art of Southern storytelling is at its finest, with so many of our mutual friends in town.

Lynwood is the kind of host I love to emulate, for he always makes it all look effortless and elegant and taste absolutely delicious. His style beckons guests to linger at the table and converse and laugh and regale with stories and tales from our various hometowns. And if you're lucky, he'll even play the piano at the dinner party-turned-cabaret!

I never leave Lynwood's house without asking for a recipe. Whether it was the main course, the dessert or even the salad, I find the need to pester my pal for the recipe. One such dish was a rice salad that he told me could be great as a pasta salad too. I've served it at several get-togethers and feel honored to tell my guests that it is Lynwood's recipe. Considering that he's usually at the table for these dinner parties, I just point and tell my guests, "Don't thank me, thank Lynwood!"

Good friends and good recipes flavor our lives and feed our spirits as much as our bellies!

This recipe doubles beautifully if you're feeding a crowd. This is perfect for 4 to 6 folks as a side or the base pasta for chicken, fish or shrimp.

---

1 pound pasta (shape of your choice; I like orecchiette, or "little ear")

1/2 cup good-quality olive oil

2 small jars artichoke hearts, chopped and drained (some juice reserved for dressing)

1/2 cup reserved artichoke juice

1/2 cup chopped green onions

1/2 cup chopped green pepper

1/2 cup chopped pimento-stuffed green olives

Heaping 1/2 cup mayonnaise

Juice of 1/2 lemon

1 tablespoon capers with brine

1 teaspoon curry powder

Freshly ground black pepper

Salt (optional)

Freshly grated Parmesan cheese, for a liberal garnish

Cook the pasta al dente so it can soak up the dressing.

Toss all the ingredients, except cheese, together thoroughly in a large bowl. Lynwood recommends refrigerating for several hours for best flavor, but it is really good right after being made. Garnish liberally with freshly grated Parmesan cheese.

FLUFFY AMBROSIA

Serves 8 to 10

Ambrosia—the feast of the gods! I remember reading in middle school literature that the gods on Mount Olympus feasted on nectar and ambrosia. This puzzled me because we were just Southern folks in a small town in Georgia and had ambrosia all the time. What was so special about this deity diet? If we ate it, it couldn't be all that special, right? Well, it was not until I was at Auburn that I had what I refer to as my "fried chicken moment." This is a moment so monumental in your life that you vividly remember where you were and nearly every detail about that moment. It's a moment that shapes your actions and your way of thinking from then on.

Most everyone, in particular most Southerners, have a "fried chicken moment" upon realizing that you are hungry, your spouse is hungry, you have a family to feed or guests coming to dinner—whatever the cause—and that you have somehow managed to leave home without learning how to fry chicken . . . or make cornbread . . . or stew tomatoes and okra . . . or bake a pound cake . . . or make pimento cheese . . . or make ambrosia.

There I was at Auburn and I was hungry. Not craving pizza and beer or typical collegiate culinary fare, but I was hungry for home. I wanted a spread like Mimi and Mrs. Mary would cook—a spread that could feed Pharaoh's army and the wandering Israelites too. How had I left home and not fully grasped the level of skill and planning it took to feed my family of close friends—and feed them well!

I'd learned the basics at home, helped enough in the kitchen to know my way around and could cook just fine, but I decided then and there that I was going to fry chicken and make ambrosia. Granted, I had Mimi in my ear over the phone, but I fried chicken in my dormitory kitchen. And I learned how to cook other dishes over the phone, at home on weekends or holidays and cooked in my Southern way all through college.

Going away to college was the catalyst for me to really start cooking like Mimi and Mrs. Mary, and it also made me realize why ambrosia was a part of the divine diet—peeling and segmenting all that citrus is a chore! Those Olympian gods had devotees to make their ambrosia! Mimi and Mary did it by hand without help. After making it myself, I had a growing feeling that they, too, may be divine.

Canned citrus and pineapple in their own juice or fruit juice is perfect for ambrosia and saves major time, especially if you're making it for the whole herd. I reserve all the juice from the jars and cans to add to the ambrosia later or as a marinade for pork or chicken. The brands jarred in glass or plastic in fruit juice are the best!

Whether ambrosia should have marshmallows is a big debate in the South, just about as big as whether it should be just citrus and tropical fruit or if apples are allowed. Nuts or no nuts? With cream or just fruit juice? I take the stance that ambrosia is perfect any way. If you have a problem with that, take it up with Zeus and Aphrodite.

---

1 cup whipping cream

3/4 cup sour cream

1 tablespoon sugar

2 cans grapefruit, drained (one regular grapefruit, one ruby red if available)

2 jars Mandarin oranges, drained

2 jars/cans pineapple tidbits or chunks, drained

1 jar maraschino cherries, drained and halved

2 apples, one green one red, chopped

1 cup chopped, toasted, and lightly salted pecans

1 heaping cup baby marshmallows

1 heaping cup frozen coconut

In a large chilled glass or metal bowl, whip together the creams and sugar to form stiff peaks. Mix the whipped creams with the fruits, pecans, marshmallows, and coconut. Allow the flavors to combine for best taste—at least a couple hours or overnight.

MILE-HIGH CORNBREAD

Makes a large skillet

Golden hued cornbread reflects further the steeping of Southern tradition for the New Year's menu. Along with luck and money from the black-eyed peas and greens, good fortune from the golden cornbread should be with us all through the year.

Granddaddy always adds a pinch more baking soda to his pan of cornbread to make it fluffier—the soda along with the self-rising cornmeal fosters mile-high, billowy pans. Plus, you must have Mile-High Cornbread to soak up the pot likker from the Lucky Money!

I use a 2 to 1 ratio for my cornbread—you can reverse it to make more of a cake-like bread or keep it mealy with the corn meal as the larger portion. This makes enough for a very large skillet of cornbread or can be divided between two pans. Y'all enjoy! And about "y'all" enjoying: there is controversy about adding sugar to cornbread and it remaining authentically Southern, as adding sugar is considered more a northern style. Whether it's "y'all" or "yous guys" making and eating it, I trust everyone will enjoy!

---

3 tablespoons bacon grease (for preheating the skillet)

$\frac{1}{3}$ cup vegetable oil, plus 3 tablespoons more for pan if not using bacon grease

3 cups self-rising cornmeal

1 $\frac{1}{2}$ cups all-purpose flour

1 tablespoon baking soda

3 eggs

2 cups buttermilk, plus add a splash or two more if batter is too thick

1 tablespoon sugar or honey

Preheat oven to 400 degrees F. Grease iron skillet with bacon grease (or oil) and let the skillet get hot in the oven.

Mix all the ingredients together into a batter and pour into the hot iron skillet. This helps form a crispy edge.

Bake for 20 to 22 minutes, or until golden brown. Serve with butter, honey butter, orange butter, apple butter, dunked in collard greens or as a snack on its own.

MASHED SWEET POTATOES

Serves 6 to 10

This dish is exactly what its name says it is. After baking the sweet potatoes until they are tender and soft all the way through, mash them and add to them as you see fit. They are delicious mashed on their own or mixed with a little cream, butter or buttermilk. Chicken stock is scrumptious splashed into the sweet potatoes. For a sweet version, sprinkle with brown sugar mixed with a little vanilla and top with sweetened coconut and toasted pecans. I love that sweet potatoes can be juxtaposed with savory stocks, salty ham or nuts, or they can go along with fellow sweet flavors.

4 medium to large sweet potatoes

2 tablespoons vegetable oil

Toppings of your choice

Preheat oven to 350 degrees F. Rub sweet potatoes with vegetable oil and wrap in tin foil.

Bake on the center rack, in an iron skillet or on a cookie sheet for 60 to 90 minutes, depending on the size of your potatoes. They need to be soft all the way through.

Unwrap from the foil and remove and discard the potato skins. Mash the potatoes together in a large bowl. Season and top as you see fit.

BOURBON MUSTARD SAUCE

Enough for 2 pork tenderloins

1 shallot, chopped

1 tablespoon minced garlic

1 tablespoon olive oil

2 cups good bourbon

3/4 cup grainy mustard

2 tablespoons Dijon mustard

3/4 cup apple cider

1 tablespoon honey

1/4 teaspoon coarse salt

1/2 teaspoon cracked black pepper

In a medium pot, lightly sauté the shallot and garlic in olive oil. Once they are translucent, add the bourbon and scrape any brown bits from the bottom of the pot. Add the mustards, apple cider, honey, salt, and pepper and allow to reduce by a third or no more than a half.

Ladle sauce over servings of roasted pork, onions, and apples or any other roasted vegetables or cabbage.

ROASTED PORK TENDERLOIN WITH BOURBON MUSTARD SAUCE

Serves 6 to 8

Pork tenderloin is my favorite cut of meat for any occasion. It has such a delicious flavor naturally that you can hardly find a better cut! Its flexibility enables it to be dressed up for a special high-end event, or it is just fine for everyday suppers.

Southerners eat pork on New Year's Day because swine move forward when searching for food—they don't scratch backwards, like farm and game fowl do. Chalk it up to superstition —similarly as to why we paint our porch ceilings haint blue—or to tradition, such as wearing white only after Easter and before Labor Day, eating fried catfish on heirloom Limoges and wearing our Sunday best to collegiate football games. We are a culture of phenomenas, right down to our food—not to mention our pageantry for crowning queens of rivers, regions and ripe produce.

As we move forward with each New Year, may we always have a good piece of pork to prompt us onward and ahead in life, always in Southern style.

---

2 pork tenderloins (about 3 pounds)

¼ cup olive oil

1 tablespoon salt

1 tablespoon black pepper

2 red or Vidalia onions, quartered

2 green apples, cored and quartered

¾ cup apple cider

Preheat the oven to 400 degrees F and pat the tenderloins dry with paper towels.

Lather the tenderloins in olive oil and sprinkle with half the salt and pepper.

In an iron skillet or oven-safe pan, first sear the tenderloins for up to 2 minutes on each side. Fill the pan with the onions, apples, and apple cider and bake in the oven for 20 to 25 minutes, tenting with tin foil for the last 10 minutes.

Remove from the oven and tent with tin foil to keep warm.

SWEET-AND-SOUR BRAISED RED CABBAGE

Serves 6 to 10

I don't know why it is exactly, but I love sweet and sour flavors with cabbage. Maybe it's because cabbage has crisp bitterness itself and can be slightly sweet, too, when braised or roasted. Red cabbage cooks down so beautifully and is a lovely contrast with the other items on the New Year's menu.

If by chance you have any leftovers, this cabbage is a great addition to a vegetable soup or is good with lentils or sausage!

1 small onion or large shallot, chopped

2 pieces bacon, chopped

1 cup apple cider vinegar

1 head red cabbage, shredded or julienned

2 tablespoons (1/4 stick) butter

1/4 cup packed dark brown sugar

2 cups chicken stock

Salt and pepper

In a large Dutch oven or lidded pot, brown the onion with the bacon. It is okay if the bacon is not fully browned—it has rendered plenty of flavor and will cook further with the cabbage.

Add the vinegar and deglaze the bottom of the pot. Then add the cabbage, butter, and sugar, and stir together until the sugar has dissolved. Add the chicken stock and simmer covered for 15 minutes. Season with salt and pepper to taste.

The cabbage may retain some crunch but will continue to soften as it sits in the juice.

GOAT CHEESE CHEESECAKE WITH SOUR CREAM CARAMEL SAUCE

Serves 10 to 12

My baby sister, Meredith, has become quite the baker in our family. One of her specialties is this Goat Cheese Cheesecake.

I am a goner when it comes to sweet and salty combinations. A sprinkling of sea salt on freshly baked chocolate chip cookies, sweet and salty toasted pecans, sea salt and caramel ice cream—and now this cake! The goat cheese has that fantastic tang about it that I so enjoy. Plus, it is not too sweet, either. The crust is a sweet-and-salty-lover's delight with pretzels and cinnamon cookies in its constitution.

I can't help but be proud of Mere—she has come into the kitchen about the same age I did and has a knack for desserts. I'll gladly hand over the baking portion of feeding the family and entertaining to her, and after trying her cheesecake, y'all will know why! And did I mention—there's a caramel sauce too?

FOR THE CRUST:

1 cup cinnamon cookies (we use the alphabet ones from Trader Joe's)

1 cup pretzel crumbs—take pretzels and bust them into crumbs by hand or in the food processor

1/2 cup sugar

3/4 cup (1 1/2 sticks) salted butter, room temperature

Lightly grease the bottom and sides of an 8-inch springform pan.

Pulse the cinnamon cookies in the food processor and remove. Pulse the pretzels too—but I like to leave a few pretzel chunks in the mix.

Combine the crumbs, sugar and butter in the food processor. This should result in an even texture with just a few larger pretzel crumbs.

Press the crust mixture into the bottom and up the sides of the prepared pan.

Preheat the oven to 325 degrees F.

Whip the cheeses using the paddle attachment of a stand mixer or with a hand mixer until fluffy. Beat in the sugar and continue beating until the mixture is light and fluffy.

FOR THE FILLING:

12 ounces goat cheese, room temperature

4 ounces cream cheese, room temperature

3/4 cup sugar

5 eggs

1 1/2 cups heavy cream

1 teaspoon vanilla

Add the eggs one at a time, beating them well into the mixture after each addition. Stir in the cream. If any lumps remain, give it another few beats with the paddle or, if desired, strain it through a sieve.

Pour the cheese filling into the crust-lined pan and bake at 325 for 1 hour. After the hour has passed, turn off the oven and leave the cheesecake in for an additional hour.

Remove cheesecake from the oven and allow it to come to room temperature. Next, chill the cheesecake for at least 4 hours in the refrigerator or overnight.

Slice into wedged pieces and top with Sour Cream Caramel Sauce. You can garnish with additional pretzel bites, cookie crumbs, or both!

continued >

GOAT CHEESE CHEESECAKE WITH SOUR CREAM CARAMEL SAUCE
(CONTINUED)

TOPPING:

This is an additional sweet and salty concoction to delight in! The caramel sauce is sour cream based and not overly sweet. It is perfect with the tangy, sweet and salty cheesecake and, quite frankly, is perfect with just about anything— apples, pineapple, grapes, pears, angel food cake, ice cream or lapped up by the spoonful!

1 cup sour cream

³/₄ cup Caramel Sauce (recipe follows)

Mix together well.

CARAMEL SAUCE

1 cup sugar

Stick of butter

³/₄ cup heavy cream

1 ¹/₂ teaspoons good vanilla

¹/₂ teaspoon salt

In a medium saucepan, heat the sugar over medium heat until it turns golden.

Stir constantly until all the sugar is dissolved and beginning to turn a darker shade of golden—more so amber.

Turn the heat to low and add the butter—stirring to combine. Fair warning: it will foam up, but keep stirring.

Next, add the heavy cream, vanilla, and salt, stirring to combine. For the next 5 to 10 minutes, stir constantly until it all comes together and looks like caramel sauce.

Pour the sauce into a Mason jar and let it come to room temperature. It will store in the refrigerator for two weeks—if it lasts that long!

JULIE'S SPICED CARROT CAKE

Makes 3 (9-inch) layers or 1 large sheet cake

When our father remarried, our new stepmother knew just what to do to win our hearts—she made a cake! Julie made her Spiced Carrot Cake and brought it to our first family trip to Cumberland Island—an undeveloped, natural habitat of spectacular Georgia flora and fauna, antebellum ruins and the enchanting Greyfield Inn. If she couldn't win us over at Cumberland—and with a cake—then there was little hope! One bite of the most delicious desserts we had ever tasted amid some of the most beautiful scenery in Georgia and we were smitten with Julie! She learned that food is the way to the Farmer children's hearts.

Stepmother sometimes has a negative connotation, but we three Farmer children have never thought of Julie as anything but a positive addition to our family. She is a blessing and a healing member of our family. I am forever grateful for her in our lives.

At their wedding, I asked Daddy if Julie was nervous. He said, "Well, she's never had children and now she has three!" I walked up to Julie, gave her a big hug and said, "Don't worry, we are all three potty trained! And, now that you're in the family, can I get the carrot cake recipe? Ha!"

---

4 eggs

2 cups sugar

1 cup vegetable or canola oil

2 cups sifted all-purpose flour

2 teaspoon cinnamon

$1/2$ teaspoon ground cloves

$1/2$ teaspoon salt

2 teaspoons baking soda

4 cups grated carrots

Splash of pineapple juice—about a tablespoon

Preheat the oven to 350 degrees F. Grease three 9-inch round cake pans or a 9 x 13-inch pan.

Beat eggs and add sugar. Then add oil and continue to beat. Sift together the flour, cinnamon, cloves, salt, and soda. Add dry ingredients to the wet ones and blend. Fold in the grated carrots and pineapple juice.

Spread the batter evenly into prepared pan(s). Bake 25 to 30 minutes at 350 and test for doneness with a toothpick in the center after 25 minutes.

continued >

CREAM CHEESE FROSTING

Makes enough for a 9 x 13 cake; double the recipe if making a three-layer version

I am not a huge icing or frosting person—more of a purist when it comes to cake. I like cake: pound cake, angel food, chocolate—plain cake. Unless the icing or frosting is something so good that it enhances the cake, not fighting it. Cream cheese icing takes the cake here—pun intended.

1 stick good-quality butter (I like Plugra European-style best; Kerrygold Irish works well too. Add a little salt if using unsalted)

2 (8-ounce) packages cream cheese

Powdered sugar to taste (a whole box is way too much)

1 tablespoon good-quality vanilla extract (just enough to smell and to color the icing slightly)

Beat butter and cream cheese together. Add salt if needed, sugar, and vanilla and blend well. Beat until fluffy.

You can make the frosting the day before baking the cake so frosting can stiffen up a little. Keep it in the fridge and then put it on the counter for an hour or so before frosting the cake.

I make extra frosting for a three-layer. If you are making a 9 x 13-inch pan, you won't need this much, so just use what is listed—unless, of course, you just want to eat it on the side!

Tweaks that make this cake divine:

- 4 cups of carrots for added moisture.

- Grate and stir in cinnamon three days prior to baking the cake. Use enough cinnamon to be able to smell it and to give the batter a brownish color. You will never use so much cinnamon at one time in your life. But the cinnamon draws out the moisture from the carrots and after the three days, you have this amazingly moist carrot mixture for the cake.

- Use toasted buttered pecans. I use Plugra European-style unsalted butter, melt it and pour it over the pecans on a baking sheet. Sprinkle with coarse salt. Toast at 350 degrees F and keep watch, as the nuts will burn the second your eye is off of them!

Baby Napp's Second Birthday Oyster Roast

My wound is geography. It is also my anchorage, my port of call. —Pat Conroy, from *The Prince of Tides*

Oh, Mr. Conroy, your words about our Southland are inked perfectly. They are apropos for many an occasion—Baby Napp's second birthday notwithstanding.

When you are a child of the Lowcountry, Bluffton's marshes, rivers and light all ebb and flow daily, consciously and subconsciously.

I reflect back on this child's little life—yet a grand one by many counts. William Napp Yelton came to us at a perfect time. Not just a perfect time, but as a "good and perfect gift." God *knew* that we would need Napp—divine knowledge gifted to a family that would be craving boundless joy, hope springing eternal, and the precious love of a child. Napp's never-ceasing glee has delighted all of us. What was in store in the coming months after Napp's arrival—the bittersweet giving and taking sing-song of life—further proved the balm of healing a baby can certainly bring.

In a moment in time when celebrating seemed a distant memory from days before loss, the contagious spirit instilled in us all from our Mimi and Mama began to reignite with the thought of celebrating Napp! What would be better than rejoicing in this Lowcountry boy than with an oyster roast and fixin's from his Georgia roots! Every day, I wonder with selfish hope if Maggie and Zach will call and say, "Guess what, Brubbs, we're moving back to Perry!" And every time I am in Bluffton, I see the sun set over the May River and watch the cadence of light and sky over the marshes turn the light into liquid. I taste the salt air as it fills my lungs with sulfurous perfume delectable only to us Southerners soulfully surrendered to the Lowcountry's spell. I know, too, that these salty airs rise from brackish waters filling our bellies with jewels of the river and sea. I taste and see and inhale the Carolina Lowcountry and know that the particular call from my sister and brother-in-law is not coming anytime soon.

So, we must go to them. And gladly so. We'll roast oysters, pile chicken salad upon platters, fill bowls with barbeque and serve pans of pimento cheese. As Mr. Conroy also said, "There are no ideas in the South, just barbeque." I couldn't agree more!

Y'all enjoy a journey to Bluffton with these recipes and images from Baby Napp's second birthday. As in true Southern tradition, we'll probably keep calling him Baby Napp well into his forties. We can't help our ways down here; we're wounded by geography, bound by tradition and must serve chicken salad, pimento cheese and barbeque at every event.

Happy Birthday, Baby Napp! Uncle Brubbs loves you to the moon and back and back again! And then back again and again!

MENU

Pirate's Treasure

"Let's Set Sail" Shooters

Creamy Blueberry Salad

Cornmeal-Dusted
Fried Oysters

Dutch Oven Green
Bean and Potato Salad

Lemon Spinach
Pasta Salad

Carolina-Style Mustard BBQ
with Wickles Pickled Veggies

Chicken Salad Sliders
with Pickled Veggies

Chocolate Delight

PIRATE'S TREASURE

Serves a few or a gang

This snack is terrific for the kids—if they're lucky enough to have a bite or two before the adults devour all the treasure! We planned to have snacks for the kiddos and grown-ups at Napp's party, but this is a snack, really, for all to enjoy! We served it up in an old tole chest I've had for years—an antique store score and a treasure itself!

Mix together your favorite snacks. These are my go-tos.

1 cup Goldfish

1 cup small pretzels

1 cup M&Ms

1 cup crunchy cereal

1 cup granola

1 cup dried fruit

1 cup nuts

Combine all ingredients. This sweet and salty rhythm is a great snack for kids of all ages! Serve the pirate's mix in the coolest container you can find.

"LET'S SET SAIL" SHOOTERS

Makes 12

My sisters and I are not necessarily crafty cooks. We like to cook and we like to be creative, but culinary craftiness is not our forte. However, Jell-O, orange candy slices and a paper sail—that we can handle! Maggie made the sailboats for the party and they sailed with success for the sailors young and old!

Our grandmothers' generation used gelatin for just about everything—aspics, fluffs, salads and fruity concoctions of every shade and combo one could imagine. I'm glad we Farmer children are embracing our heritage and continuing the tradition!

When thinking about Mimi and her contemporaries and all their gelatinous salads, I can't help but crave one. Doesn't the kid in all of us still love Jell-O?

---

1 box blueberry or grape Jello-O

Orange candy slices

Follow the directions on a box of blueberry or grape Jell-O and divide the liquid among clear plastic cups. Once the Jell-O has chilled and set, top with a piece of orange candy slices and a sail—toothpick and paper triangle. Ahoy, y'all!

FARMER'S NOTE: I probably don't need to explain how to make these shooters for grownups only—haven't we all experienced the intoxicating power of vodka and Jell-O sometime in college? It's a rite of passage in the SEC, I'm afraid! I still have the fear that my parents will found out!

CREAMY BLUEBERRY SALAD

Serves 12 to 15

I love the crunch of the pistachios in this salad and the sweet-and-salty pace they set, too! The sour cream and cream cheese tame the sweetness and give a touch of tangy goodness. This salad has so many variations—strawberry, blackberry, grape and citrus versions abound. This one may be my favorite, though! Pistachios are a twist on the traditional walnuts and pecans; I even love salty Marcona almonds! A splash of fresh blueberries gives a bit of freshness to the pie filling.

2 (3-ounce) packages grape Jell-O

2 cups boiling water

1 can blueberry pie filling

1/2 cup fresh blueberries

1 can crushed pineapple, drained

FOR THE TOPPING:

1 (8-ounce) package cream cheese

1 cup sour cream

1/2 cup powdered sugar

1 teaspoon vanilla

3/4 cup crushed pistachios

In a large bowl, dissolve gelatin in boiling water. Allow to cool for 10 minutes. Stir in pie filling, blueberries, and pineapple until everything is well blended. Transfer to a 9 x 13-inch pan or divide among individual ramekins. Cover and refrigerate until the salad is partially set, about 1 hour.

To make the topping, combine the cream cheese, sour cream, sugar, and vanilla in a medium-sized bowl. Carefully spread over the gelatin and sprinkle with pistachios. Cover and refrigerate until firm.

CORNMEAL-DUSTED FRIED OYSTERS

Serves 10 to 12

The May River boasts some of the sweetest, most delectable oysters in the South. Shucked and eaten raw, barbequed, steamed, roasted, fried or broiled, there are as many ways to eat an oyster as there are Southern Jell-O recipes! We love to use a steamer to bring the briny jewel's flavor up a notch then douse with condiments of our choosing. Add hot sauce, lemon juice, and a saltine cracker and your steamed oysters are ready to shoot back and enjoy! Roasting them on a metal grate or rack over a bonfire or fire pit is a fabulous fashion for oysters too! Whether steaming or roasting, plan on each batch taking about 8 to 10 minutes, or until the shells begin to pop open.

Now, I stand by the rule for us especially in the Deep South to eat raw oysters only in months with an "r" in their name. This old adage stems from not eating oysters May through August, the hottest months. Yet this doesn't prevent me from frying them!

For frying oysters, cornmeal is the ticket! The grainy grit adheres perfectly to the oysters and doesn't take away from their flavor; in fact, cornmeal complements the oysters rather than masking their flavor, as other breadings can. I hope y'all enjoy these as much as I do! This recipe will feed several folks. You can reduce it by half or double it if the whole tribe is coming over—which is usually the case when y'all are frying oysters!

Corn oil for frying

3 cups yellow cornmeal

1 ½ teaspoons salt

1 heaping tablespoon black pepper

6 dozen oysters, shucked and drained

In a large Dutch oven or a deep fryer with wire basket, heat the oil until very hot, 370 to 375 degrees F.

While heating the oil, mix the cornmeal, salt, and pepper on a dredging board or long sheet of waxed paper. Drain the oysters and dredge them in the cornmeal mixture; be sure to coat each oyster well.

Use a slotted spoon, wire skimmer, or frying spoon to lower the oysters into the Dutch oven, 8 or so at a time in a single layer. Fry for about 2 minutes, or until uniformly golden. Allow the oil to reheat between batches. Keep frying in one-layer batches and remove from the oil onto paper towels. Serve with Mimi's Sauce (page 44), cocktail sauce, tartar sauce, or rémoulade (page 51).

DUTCH OVEN GREEN BEAN AND POTATO SALAD

Serves 6

The reason I call this dish a "salad" is because I make it very often as a side dish for beef filets, pork and grilled chicken, and the leftovers are still so good even when cold that I then call them a "salad" rather than the unappealing term "leftovers."

I do love a one-pot wonder kind of dish, and this is certainly a stove to table to picnic to party to potluck to whatever sort of thing! I love this salad warm, room temp or cold. Thus why it is such a great dish to bring to a dinner on the grounds or serve at a picnic. The sauce that the butter, oil and sour cream creates is nothing short of marvelous. Trust me on this one: you'll be scraping every ounce off your plate and asking for more!

---

4 tablespoons (½ stick) butter

3 tablespoons olive oil

1½ pounds Baby Dutch yellow potatoes, fingerlings, or other small potatoes

1 teaspoon salt

1 teaspoon pepper

2 Farmer's handfuls whole green beans, trimmed

1½ cups sour cream

Melt the butter in a large Dutch oven or heavy-bottomed pot. Add the oil and allow to warm until you can smell it (a delicious scent!).

Add the whole potatoes, salt, and pepper and toss well, coating the potatoes. Cover the pot tightly and cook over low heat for about 20 to 30 minutes, or until the potatoes are just tender when poked with a small knife or fork. Occasionally stir quickly so as to not allow too much steam to escape, or shake the pot to prevent the bottom potatoes from burning.

Add the beans and sour cream. Turn off the heat and allow the potatoes to steam for another 5 to 7 minutes. Delicious served hot, warm or cold.

FARMER'S NOTE: *For some seasonal freshness, add some rosemary, parsley, dill, sage, scallions, green onions, or ramps!*

LEMON SPINACH PASTA SALAD

Serves 4 to 6

Another dish I love warm or cold, my Lemon Spinach Pasta Salad is also easy. I tell folks that if you can boil water, you can make this dish. Seriously, cooking the pasta is the only "cooking" required.

My sisters both clamor for this salad. Maggie loves the sun-dried tomatoes and Meredith loves the Parmesan-coated noodles and spinach. You can see them eat their respective flavors first from their plates then switch plates with one another! It's like watching a synchronized ballet!

I always double the recipe since I'm usually feeding a crowd, but I also love how good this dish is left over. It is the perfect base for grilled chicken, poached fish or as the foundation for shrimp, scallops or fried oysters. It is a simple, clean and elegant complement to so many entrées that this dish has become a vital part of my culinary repertoire. I hope the same for y'all!

---

1 pound penne pasta

$^3/_4$ cup good olive oil, plus more for drizzling

3 lemons—two for juicing and one sliced

$^1/_2$ teaspoon Dijon mustard

$^1/_2$ teaspoon minced garlic

$1^1/_2$ teaspoons salt

$1^1/_2$ teaspoons pepper

$^3/_4$ cup finely grated fresh Parmesan, Romano, or Asiago cheese

1 heaping cup pine nuts, gently warmed or toasted

2 cups fresh spinach

1 cup sun-dried tomatoes, julienned

Cook the pasta al dente as directed on the package. This will allow the noodles to soak up the other flavors. Drain and add the noodles to a large salad bowl; drizzle with olive oil.

In a Mason jar, bowl or measuring cup, whisk together the lemon juice, $^3/_4$ cup olive oil, mustard, garlic, salt, and pepper.

Toss the warm pasta with the dressing and add the cheese, pine nuts, spinach and tomatoes. The heat from the pasta will gently wilt the spinach. Toss well, garnish with lemon slices, and serve warm or chilled.

CAROLINA-STYLE MUSTARD BBQ WITH WICKLES PICKLED VEGGIES

Figure $\frac{1}{2}$ pound per person

Oh, barbeque! Each state and even county, for that matter, has a claim to preparing it. Smoking and rubbing and sauces and cuts of meat (BBQ means pork in the Deep South and usually beef in Texas) all vary across state lines and through bloodlines, too. All I know is that I love barbeque—especially with a couple of crucial pickles. For me, a mustardy barbeque sauce with finely chipped pork is probably my favorite, though I haven't ever turned down a smoky dry-rubbed brisket or bourbon-glazed pork any time I can think of . . . I digress.

I think every Southern gentleman should know how to smoke a Boston Butt, chip it finely and serve it with his favorite BBQ sauce. Just think how many friends you'll have if you possess this prowess! Grilling, smoking and cooking outdoors is a great time for the menfolk to gather and enjoy some time together. Plus, this time gives us the opportunity to tell our fishing and hunting stories over and over again—the fish growing larger and the points higher on the buck with each telling!

With varying styles of BBQ sauces flowing across the South as rivers of concocted spices across pork shoulders and briskets, it is hard to pick a very favorite. I still, though, lean towards a mustardy sauce, maybe because such sauces of the like—such as Mrs. Griffin's made in nearby Macon, Georgia—have run down the Ocmulgee River, south of the Fall Line and into my home. Or even Melvin's out of Charleston, South Carolina, whose peppery mustard base has been a choice for years as well. With Napp growing up in the Carolina Lowcountry, I feel that the mustardy sauce for BBQ is just perfect.

I love the pickled heat of Wickles Pickles and especially love Wickles veggies! These make wonderful additions to a BBQ sandwich or plate. I think the vinegary goodness with a gentle heat is perfectly suited for a mustardy BBQ sauce. I discovered Wickles at a tailgate while at Auburn and am thrilled that they can be found across the South in just about every grocery store and gourmet market too! I can also boast that I have probably eaten my weight in their pickles, pickled veggies and okra—and don't forget their relish for sausage and hot dogs.

MY STANDBY METHOD FOR BOSTON BUTT

Season a Boston Butt to taste. This may include an array of spices, rubs and herbs or simply salt and pepper. Either way, the smoke and natural flavor of this cut is the magical and delicious bit.

Wrap your seasoned shoulder—that's what it is actually—loosely in tinfoil and smoke it in a smoker, grill, barbeque pit, fire pit, oven, or whatever floats your boat at a low, smoky heat: 200–250 degrees for about 8 to 12 hours, depending on the size and weight of the pork shoulder. I follow the $1\frac{1}{2}$ hours per pound at 225 formula.

Once the meat is sufficiently cooked (to about 190–205 finished temperature), fantastically pink smoke rings will ensue. The pork may literally be pulled away from the bone and doused or dipped in barbeque sauce or chipped finely and then flooded in a river of sauce.

CAROLINA-STYLE MUSTARD BBQ SAUCE

2 cups yellow mustard

1 teaspoon dry mustard

1 heaping cup ketchup

2 tablespoon Worcestershire sauce

1 tablespoon dark brown sugar

$\frac{1}{2}$ cup white vinegar or apple cider vinegar

1 tablespoon liquid smoke

A few dashes of pepper sauce

1 tablespoon garlic powder

Several dashes of Nature's Seasons

1 teaspoon salt

1 tablespoon black pepper

Over low heat, mix all the ingredients together and thin with vinegar to desired thickness. Season further to taste. Serve with chipped pork, beef, or chicken.

CHICKEN SALAD SLIDERS WITH PICKLED VEGGIES

Serves 4

As you'll find with barbeque, chicken salad can take top billing at just about any Southern event. As I always say, "married or buried, you'll have chicken salad."

Also, if you could count the grains of sand from New Orleans to Biloxi to Gulf Shores to Charleston and back, you may have just started on the quantitative figure of Southern chicken salad recipes. As a friend of mine says in her fantastically Southern tongue-in-cheek tone, "That's a great start, shug."

This chicken salad recipe is a standby for us because we can pick it up anytime we have a party (wedding, funeral, visiting dignitary) from Georgia Bob's BBQ. Thankfully, Georgia Bob's has franchised and you can satisfy your desire for their chicken salad just about anywhere in Middle Georgia proper! It has the right amount of sweetness to tame the salty pecans and the right amount of crunch from the celery. Their recipe remains a secret but has become an institution at any celebration in our area.

My version is inspired by Georgia Bob's slightly sweet chicken salad, which to me is the winning ticket to the dish. Chicken salad is so often savory that when lightly sweetened and paired with hearty amounts of celery and some pecans, you find an equilibrium so satisfying.

---

2 tablespoons fresh lemon juice

$1/2$–$3/4$ cup mayonnaise

$1/2$ teaspoon sugar or $3/4$ teaspoon honey

1 teaspoon salt

1 teaspoon pepper

1 teaspoon celery seed

3 $1/2$ cups finely diced cooked chicken (about 3-4 boneless chicken breasts; I like mine baked with olive oil, salt, and pepper)

1 heaping cup finely diced celery

$1/2$ cup chopped pecans, or slivered or finely chopped almonds

12 mini slider rolls

In a small bowl, combine the lemon juice, mayonnaise, sugar, salt, pepper, and celery seed. In a medium to large bowl, toss the chicken, celery, and nuts. Serve on mini slider rolls with your favorite pickles.

This recipe is easy to double, triple or multiply in any quantity.

PICKLED VEGGIES

Makes 5 pints

2 pounds fresh veggies, e.g., small okra, cauliflower or broccoli florets, or carrots

1 quart distilled white vinegar

2 tablespoons salt

2 tablespoons sugar

1 tablespoon Tabasco sauce

1 tablespoon Worcestershire sauce

5 cloves garlic, peeled

1 tablespoon dried dill

1 tablespoon mustard seed

5 small whole peppers—mild or hot, depending on your heat tolerance

Wash and pat veggies dry. If using okra, soak in cold water after washing for about an hour. This helps keep the okra from being slimy when added to the warm pickling juice.

Sterilize and keep hot 5 pint jars with their corresponding lids.

In a medium-sized pot, mix the remaining ingredients together and bring to a boil. Remove and reserve the peppers and garlic.

Distribute the veggies of your choosing evenly among the jars, with a pepper and a garlic clove.

Carefully fill the hot jars with the boiling pickling juice and seal. Store in a cool, dry place.

FARMER'S NOTE: For a good-looking arrangement of pickled okra in the jar, pack it with one pod up and one pod down. This makes a pretty scene in the jar.

CHOCOLATE DELIGHT

Serves 10

This simple recipe holds a special place in my heart. Mama made this for us quite often growing up, and it was one of the first dishes I made for my college Supper Club at Auburn. That first time I made it, I followed Mama's instructions perfectly. My Chocolate Delight was fine but wasn't the same as hers. I felt like my shortbread crust was weaker than hers.

My friends all thought it was delicious, though, and I thanked them and relayed the compliments back to Mama. I had to ask her if she may have withheld anything or a tip from me. "Double the crust, honey—double the crust."

That expression became mine and Mama's running joke about so many things. If we toured a lovely home, we would say to each other, "They doubled the crust on this one!" Or if we saw a camellia or Confederate Rose or wisteria blooming out of control, we would say, "That bush has doubled its crust!" We used the phrase often and laughed every time we said it! This turn of phrase became our way of proclaiming something as "high cotton," in our opinion. But it has come to mean more to me since Mama's passing—meaning that I have an inheritance of love and legacy to uphold beyond her life.

Now, for me, to "double the crust" is not necessarily to make something grander or better or somehow posed as something it really is not. To "double the crust" means to give the task at hand, the endeavor of the season or the project de jour—especially if investing in another person—that little bit of extra gusto, fervor or heart.

Mama loved wholeheartedly and she loved lavishly. She "doubled the crust" with her children, family, students and dearest friends; and sometimes, that's just what folks need. Sometimes folks just need someone to give them a little bit more—maybe that is love, confidence, affirmation or simply a safe, wonderful place to call home. Mama certainly did that for us—especially since a little extra shortbread crust can go a long way.

FOR THE DOUBLED CRUST:

2 cups of all-purpose flour

1 cup (2 sticks) butter, room temperature

2 tablespoons brown sugar

1/4 teaspoon vanilla

1/2–3/4 cup finely chopped pecans

FIRST LAYER:

1 (8-ounce) package cream cheese, room temperature

1 cup powdered sugar

1 heaping cup whipped cream (homemade whipped cream, which makes a huge difference, y'all)

SECOND LAYER:

2 (3.9-ounce) packages instant chocolate pudding

3 cups whole milk

TOPPING:

2 cups homemade whipped cream

Chopped pecans, for garnish (optional)

Preheat oven to 350 degrees F.

For the crust, in a bowl mix together the flour, butter, brown sugar, vanilla and pecans until mixture resembles cookie dough. Spread into the bottom of a 9 x 13-inch glass baking dish. Bake for about 20 minutes, or until lightly browned. Cool completely, about an hour. This is the hardest part because this "shortbread" is tough to resist eating immediately.

For the first layer, mix together the cream cheese and powdered sugar until well blended. Add 1 cup of the whipped cream and incorporate everything together. Spread this first layer over the cooled crust.

For the second layer, mix the pudding with the milk until slightly thickened; this should take about 3 minutes. Carefully spread over the cream cheese layer. As this dessert sits and sets, the cream cheese layer and the chocolate pudding layer marbleize.

Spread the remaining cup or so of whipped cream on top of the chocolate pudding. Cover and refrigerate for 12 to 24 hours. The longer it can set, the better! Garnish with more chopped pecans if desired.

Scoop and serve! It can be cut into squares, but I find a deep dish of Chocolate Delight simply is best scooped and dumped onto the plate! Piled high, of course!

FARMER'S NOTE: *This crust recipe is like a pecan sandy and is great as a shortbread or sandy-style cookie on its own. It is great as a crust for other desserts too!*

Sunday Night at Home

Sunday nights are not necessarily *the* celebratory night of the week. Friday and Saturday take on the lion's share of parties, receptions, celebrations and social engagements, as the weekend's high rollers and the "school" nights of the week usually keep us accountable to work and school and schedules and routines. Then we find that Sunday nights are all too often filled with traveling home from weekend getaways or leaving home for business treks, or we're simply exhausted.

On weekends home from Auburn, I would take advantage of the time change across the river and leave early Monday morning, allowing one more night at home, uninterrupted by the logistics of life and the rigors of schedules. I am one of those souls who needs a night at home, to recharge with my family, close friends or even by myself and to gear up for the coming week.

Breakfast for supper is a true favorite of mine. Now, y'all, I can eat breakfast for any meal, but I cannot eat any meal for breakfast. Traditional breakfast foods are de rigueur for breakfast proper for me, but give me eggs and grits any time of day! I'll take oatmeal for lunch or dinner and, of course, bacon and biscuits are completely acceptable at any meal with just about anything!

Preparing and serving a big breakfast on Monday morning, let alone any other day of the week, would be a miraculous feat. Our weekday breakfasts are lucky to even exist past coffee or tea. Yet, on the weekends, the luxury of even a slight slowing of time affords the opportunity for breakfast. Still, having breakfast for a

Sunday supper is just that much more comforting and bracing to cap the weekend and prepare us for the next week.

My family has celebrated Sunday night with "breakfast for supper" for as long as I can remember. Mimi could whip up fried eggs and grits with bacon and biscuits and we would devour the spread like ducks on a June bug. Mama kept the tradition and we still do, too. There is a level of comfort that only a skillet of eggs, a pot of grits and a pan of biscuits can afford. Little did I know that this family tradition would take root in the soil of my soul and grow steadily throughout my life into a cherished memory of time together before life's sway commanded our schedules away from home.

Sunday nights are now sacred to me. They were when I was a child, too, but I did not recognize it. The reflection on home and childhood from the stance of adulthood always holds a gravitas greater than our childish perspective. To me, this is the one night of the week I feel should not be tainted with "real life." Not that I am some romantic or out of touch, but I am more so a real person who needs a moment to focus on the importance of scrambling eggs. I trust I am in good company with this thinking.

The healing power of food forces us to stop, refuel and simply be still. It is the stillness that relaxes our minds, fills our bellies and in turn recharges our spirits. May your Sunday nights be filled with tradition, comfort and time together.

MENU

Sweet-and-Salty Oatmeal
with Fresh and Dried Fruit

Roasted Garlic and
Chive Grits

Mushroom and Spinach
Frittata with Goat Cheese

Pimento Cheese Eggs

Brown Sugar
and Rosemary Bacon

Southern-Style
Waldorf Salad

Uncle Gerry's Biscuits

Earl Grey Lattes

SWEET-AND-SALTY OATMEAL WITH FRESH AND DRIED FRUIT

Serves 4

Growing up, whenever I heard the tale of Goldilocks and the Three Bears, I craved oatmeal—that's what I was told "porridge" was. "Porridge is like oatmeal, hon," I can remember Mimi telling me. "Why did they eat porridge, Mimi?" I would ask. "Because, love, they didn't have grits."

I loved oatmeal as a child and envied Goldilocks for finding that particular bowl of porridge that was "just right." In the fashion Mimi believed the Three Bears would've taken theirs, she would make us "porridge" and give us a buffet of toppings to make our very own bowls "just right." I loved doctoring up my oatmeal with apples, cinnamon, raisins, other dried fruits, pecans and honey. That was, until I developed a bizarre allergy to oats—oats and apples. My favorite nursery rhyme meal was blown away like the little pig's straw house!

Thankfully, I outgrew the allergy, but I had a few years sans a bowl of porridge, thus leaving me a waxing appetite for oatmeal topped with all the accompaniments. Now that I am the one making the oatmeal, I want to re-create the fun we had pretending we were nursery-rhyme characters but suitable for grown-up taste. For me, the complementing singsong of sweet—salty, crunchy—creamy and fresh—dried is the best. Oatmeal is a perfect vehicle to deliver these flavors.

Make a big pot of this oatmeal, season lightly with cinnamon and sugar and top it off with a varying sundry of fruit and nuts for your family, a dinner party, a brunch or to eat for meals through the week! May we never lose the imagination of our childhood, especially when a nursery rhyme launches the inspiration for such a delicious dish!

---

4 cups water

1/2 teaspoon salt

2 cups extra-thick rolled oats (I love Bob's Red Mill)

2 cinnamon sticks

1 tablespoon good-quality vanilla

2 tablespoons butter

1/2 cup packed dark brown sugar

1 cup milk (whole or 2%)

Garnishes—chopped apples, dried figs, raisins, salted pecans or walnuts or sunflower seeds

In a medium to large pot, bring the water to boil with the salt and add the oats and cinnamon sticks. Cook on medium heat for 10 to 15 minutes, or until desired consistency; I like my oatmeal thicker and oats more prominent rather than mushy.

Add the vanilla, butter, brown sugar, and milk and stir. Allow the oatmeal to sit for a couple of minutes, then garnish with fruits and nuts of your choice. The sweetness of the oatmeal and dried fruit with the salty seeds and nuts are delightful complements! Enjoy!

ROASTED GARLIC AND CHIVE GRITS

Serves 6 to 8 folks easily

I am member of the ranks of Southern-born and -bred children who know the comforting power of a warm bowl of grits. Mama would make us grits on the first day of school to have something in our bellies and calm our back-to-school jitters. Chicken noodle soup may heal a cold, but grits will heal the soul!

Grits are a flavor highway to connect complementary flavors. They're fabulous with seafood, as a base for cheese, bacon and green onions, and of course, a sunny-side up egg's best friend. Grits are typically always savory for Southerners and can be found on the menus of the finest Southern restaurants and in nearly every kitchen too. This particular recipe adds a sweet note to the grits—not sugary but a hint of sweet from the garlic and cream cheese.

Roasting the garlic brings out the natural sugar and caramelizes it, sweetening the cloves and making them a lovely contribution to thick, creamy grits. The garlic becomes tender and nearly melts into the grits. Adding some brightness and gentle onion flavor with the addition of chives makes this dish come to life. Serve these grits as part of a brunch or dinner buffet or as a breakfast dish itself. I love grits with salmon, shrimp or scallops too!

---

1 or 2 heads of garlic, sliced in half and roasted, about 10–12 cloves

Olive oil

4 cups water

4 cups chicken stock

1 teaspoon salt, plus a little more

2 cups good-quality grits (not instant)

2 tablespoons butter

³/₄ cup milk

1 (8-ounce) package cream cheese

Black pepper

¹/₂ cup chopped chives, for garnish

Gently roast the garlic with some olive oil until the cloves are browned and tender, about 30 minutes.

In a large pot, bring the water, stock, and 1 teaspoon salt to a boil and add the grits. Reduce heat and simmer until bubbly and creamy, about 10 to 15 minutes. Add the butter and milk and stir. Allow to cook on low heat for another 5 minutes then remove from heat.

Add the cream cheese and incorporate well; season to taste with salt and pepper. Toss in the garlic and stir again. Sprinkle with chopped chives.

MUSHROOM AND SPINACH FRITTATA WITH GOAT CHEESE

Serves 6 to 8

Growing up with chickens on the farm, we had eggs quite often. Eggs, to me, are a perfect food—perfect in their adaptability, versatility, healthy makeup and ability to be served for any meal. I could live off eggs and grits—scrambled, sunny-side up, over easy, hard-boiled, you name it! Omelets, though, I feel are a tad intimidating. I cannot flip 'em! Plus, I overstuff them and they fall apart. Now, a frittata I can handle!

If you can crack an egg, you can make a frittata. Your friends and family will think you've just attended the finest culinary school when you serve a frittata for breakfast, brunch, lunch or dinner. This combo is as easy as it is delicious. Pairing earthy mushrooms with bright spinach and then some creamy, tangy goat cheese on a soufflé-like eggy base just can't be beat!

This dish is an all-around winner, for it is as lovely as it is delicious and easy. Crack the eggs, mix the ingredients, pour them into a pan and bake! Slice into wedges and serve with grits, a salad or as a meal on its own merit—it truly merits all accolades! Y'all enjoy!

---

12 eggs

1 heaping cup sliced mushrooms (I like a mix of crimini, baby portabella, and chanterelles)

1 cup spinach leaves

³/₄ cup crumbled goat cheese

¹/₂ teaspoon salt

¹/₂ teaspoon pepper

Preheat oven to 350 degrees F.

In a large bowl, crack the eggs and beat them well until slightly frothy. Add the remaining ingredients and pour the mixture into a greased iron skillet or oven-safe skillet.

Bake for about 20 minutes, until the center is nearly done. The frittata will continue to cook for a few minutes outside the oven. Allow to cool and then slice and serve!

FARMER'S NOTE: *You can add and subtract so many things to a frittata. Peppers, onions, meats, other cheeses and herbs all make lovely additions. This can be a great way to clean out the produce bin and possibilities are limited only by your taste and creativity!*

PIMENTO CHEESE EGGS

Serves 1

This dish is the ultimate combination of two of my favorite things: pimento cheese and scrambled eggs. I like to remind folks that eggs are a liquid and turn to a solid with heat. Don't overcook them. Take them from the skillet while the slightest bit runny and they'll keep cooking for a few seconds and firm up just in time to eat!

On many an occasion, this dish is my supper. I always have eggs and pimento cheese on hand, so no matter how hectic the day, in minutes I can have a dish for supper that is filling and full of flavor! I hope y'all enjoy my favorite way to eat eggs any time of day.

3 eggs

Salt and freshly ground black pepper

2 teaspoons olive oil

Pimento Cheese (facing)

In a medium bowl, whisk the eggs together and season to taste.

In a small pan over medium-to-low heat, scramble the eggs in oil and top with a heaping tablespoon of pimento cheese.

BROWN SUGAR AND ROSEMARY BACON

You know I love sweet and salty together. Throw in some savory, too, and my taste buds reel with delight! Plus, the kitchen is enveloped in the heavenly aroma of the these ingredients with a rosemary top note. Fair warning, your neighbors may knock down the door in an attempt to taste this delicacy!

Be sure to use a hearty, thick-cut bacon to uphold the melodic dancing flavors. Benton's is one of the South's best bacons, and ham too. Ham can be treated in this same fashion. This recipe makes bacon a star as the sidekick to eggs and can be crumbled and served with grits, atop a salad, with roasted sweet potatoes or sprinkled over mashed potatoes. But the best way to eat it is to sneakily and stealthily devour a couple of slices before anyone takes notice!

1 pound good, thick-sliced bacon

3/4 cup loosely packed dark brown sugar

1/2 cup rosemary leaves stripped from the stem

Lay out a pound of bacon on lightly greased roasting pans or rimmed baking sheets. Sprinkle liberally with brown sugar and rosemary.

Bake at 350 degrees F for 10 minutes and then turn the heat up to 400 for another 5 minutes, or until desired crispiness. Save the drippings for other uses—those are liquid gold!

PEPPERY PIMENTO CHEESE

Makes about 4 cups

1 cup of finely shredded sharp cheddar cheese

1 cup of finely shredded sharp Vermont white
   cheddar cheese

1/2–3/4 cup mayonnaise

3/4 jar of Lindsay's pimento pieces with some juice
   (the juice can be used to thin out the mayo)

1 small jalapeño, chopped (don't use the seeds
   unless you want it very hot!)

1/2 cup chopped pecans, pistachios, or Marcona
   almonds

Squirt of lemon juice

Dash of Lawry's Seasoned Salt

Dash of Nature's Seasons

Pinch of cayenne pepper

1 tablespoon black pepper (this is a lot but makes
   it so good!)

Coarse ground sea salt

Shredding your own cheese makes a big difference in taste. Fold and stir cheese together with all the ingredients until blended. Serve with crackers, on sandwiches, or with veggies for dipping.

SOUTHERN-STYLE WALDORF SALAD

Serves 4

This famed salad from the Waldorf Astoria in New York, first created by the historic hotel's maître d' and not the chef, originally contained apples, celery and mayonnaise. And the recipe has remained basically the same for years! But there is always room for variation, and this version is a fresh take on the classic dish. Mimi and Mrs. Mary have both taught me to use the power of celery in my cooking. It is a clean flavor with a savory hint and a green crunch. Whether they chopped it, minced it, grated it or roasted it with onions and carrots, celery has had a presence well suited in many dishes. I especially love it grated or sliced uber thin on a mandolin.

Grating ingredients like onion, garlic, ginger, and celery gives these distinct flavors the opportunity to complement and not compete in a dish. Finely grated, these particular ingredients marinate and permeate the dish. I even like to grate some celery to use for sauces, soups, and dressings—it'll keep all week in the fridge and you might as well grate a bunch while you're at it.

The Southern spin on my Waldorf Salad begins with toasted pecans—toasted pecans in butter and sprinkled with salt. Walnuts were a later, lovely addition to the original salad. If you use walnuts, then try toasting them too. This process brings out their natural oils, enhancing the flavor tremendously. I also like to use dried and fresh forms of a fruit. In the salad, raisins and grapes give a pop of freshness along with chewy sweetness.

So, with toasted pecans, grapes and raisins, and the grated celery all together in a base of chopped tart-and-sweet apples, I felt that mayonnaise was a tad heavy to dress the dish. Greek yogurt gives the dish grounding and marries all the fruit and flavors together without competing. Now, if only I could get folks at the Waldorf to say "y'all," I'd really be changing things up!

Grating a little bit of celery is the most difficult instruction for this dish, so you hardly have an excuse not to make it for breakfast or any time of the day!

---

4 apples, chopped (I like 2 tart Granny Smiths and two sweet Fujis)

1 heaping cup buttered, salted, and lightly toasted pecans

2 tablespoons grated celery, plus additional thinly sliced for garnish

1 heaping cup grapes (green, red, or both), halved

¾ cup raisins

1½ heaping cups Greek yogurt

Mix all the ingredients together in a large bowl and serve chilled or at room temperature. Garnish with thinly sliced celery and serve on a bed of Bibb lettuce or as a fruit salad side dish.

UNCLE GERRY'S BISCUITS

Makes a baker's dozen

Biscuit making is a rite of passage for Southerners. Most of us have a designated biscuit maker in the family. For ours, it is Uncle Gerry, surprisingly enough!

Now, Mrs. Mary still makes her legendary biscuits when she cooks for Granddaddy and for special occasions for us, and her biscuits are still the very flavor of childhood and nostalgia. Uncle Gerry, in his infinite wisdom, thought someone else in the family should learn. And so he did.

Mimi stopped making biscuits years ago. She said she couldn't compete with the frozen biscuits from our local butcher shops, and rightly so—those are fantastic! But there is nothing like a made-from-scratch biscuit. Once you master the skill, you can whip out batches of biscuits at a moment's notice. The only thing better than a homemade biscuit is a homemade biscuit with honey or syrup. That, y'all, is nothing short of a divine experience.

Uncle Gerry told me that he remembered how Mimi made biscuits back in the day (he and Aunt Kathy were high school sweethearts) and decided he would be the torchbearer to continue the tradition. Part of that tradition is teaching the next generation—and my baby sister Meredith became the lucky pupil. After a few attempts at learning their technique myself, Meredith walked me through the process. Usually I'm teaching Mere about something in the kitchen; how the tables turn!

Physician by day and biscuit baker by night—I think my family is blessed to have such a combo in Uncle Gerry! Meredith and I are glad for the tutorials.

---

2 cups all-purpose flour

1 teaspoon salt

1 tablespoon baking powder

1-2 tablespoons sugar

6 tablespoons butter, frozen and cut into small cubes

¾ cup buttermilk*

Preheat oven to 450 degrees F.

In a large bowl, whisk together the dry ingredients then cut butter into flour. Add the buttermilk while working butter into the dough—working it in, not necessarily kneading it. You'll end up folding several times.

On a generously floured surface, roll out the very sticky dough and cut out biscuits with a biscuit cutter or small jar. Place biscuits on a baking sheet and cook in the center of the oven for 8 to 10 minutes for a skillet (10 to 12 for a baking sheet or round cake pan), until they turn lightly golden.

FARMER'S NOTE: *I love honey! I am a true believer in honey's properties as a remedy for many ailments and the best friend that butter can make! Granddaddy loves Golden Eagle Syrup, which is very similar to a good, thick honey. Choose your poison—ha!*

For this buttermilk, Unc likes to add 3 teaspoons white vinegar to 1 cup whole milk and allow them to sit together and thicken. Uncle Gerry adds a pinch of baking powder to the milk too. This thickening takes about 15 minutes.

EARL GREY LATTES

Makes a single serving

I don't like to drink coffee, but I will eat it. I use coffee in my chocolate cake recipe, love tiramisu and coffee-flavored ice cream. I make up for my lack of drinking coffee by drinking tea. Trust me, I know the urge for a little pick-me-up that a favorite beverage can afford. I've had friends tell me that I just don't understand their need for a cup of coffee in the morning. I just tell them that I truly do—but for me, y'all, it's genetic!

Two of my great-grandmothers only drank tea. My mimi only drank tea—hot and iced—as did my mama. My eye color came from my Daddy, but my affinity for tea came from Mama's side. In fact, Maggie and Meredith, too, do not drink coffee—the gene runs deep and wide! The rift between coffee and tea drinkers can be a chasm of greatest division, even within the same family.

My Granddaddy Napp's coffee is often used by the Georgia Department of Transportation as tar to patch roads. Daddy and Julie roast their own coffee beans, grind them and have their coffee down to a gourmet art form. Aunt Kathy has the hottest coffee known to man percolating through the day in her kitchen, but then Uncle Gerry evens out our kindred tribe by drinking hot tea.

Southerners have a sharp identity in their iced tea. Iced tea is prevalent across the country. Sweet tea is the house wine of the South. Traveling across the country for speaking engagements and book signings has been an adventure! One challenge I have faced on my travels is how to keep my constant craving for sweet tea satisfied. I cringe when servers bring sugar for me to sweeten my iced tea—don't they know that sugar won't dissolve in cold tea? But y'all know what will mix splendidly? Simple syrup.

One time, my darling friend and fellow Southern Living *Editor-at-Large Jenna Bush Hager and I were having lunch in New York. I told Jenna that I needed a glass of sweet tea, and she told me there wasn't any to be had in the Big Apple. So I asked our server if she could bring me a small pitcher of simple syrup from the bar so I could sweeten my iced tea. Jenna looked at me and said, "I've been in New York for years and have yet to get a drop of sweet tea. One lunch with James and I have gallons!"*

Taking the sweet iced tea to the coffee house is a whole other predicament. Coffee houses smell so good and purvey many hot teas too. These places I have found to be an oasis in the desert of unsweet tea, for, like a bar, they will have simple syrup too. And they also have my go-to hot tea drink—Earl Grey Lattes. I love how the natural sweetness of milk and a touch of honey can satisfy my sweet tooth and allow me to look the part while meeting friends at the coffee house.

Hot milk, a tea bag, some cinnamon, a little honey and a splash of vanilla—and the all-important foamy head that makes a latte a lot more festive than a regular cup of tea. I like to use a little immersion blender to foam up warm milk to top my Earl Grey Lattes, but I do love them sans sudsy topping too.

You may have to instruct your coffee house's barista on an Earl Grey Latte on your first order, but they'll be glad to oblige. This is an easy drink and most comforting. I hope y'all agree.

---

1 cup milk

1/2 teaspoon vanilla

1/2 teaspoon honey

1/4 teaspoon cinnamon or a cinnamon stick to soak in the warm milk or stir the tea

1 Earl Grey tea bag

Heat the milk on the stove with the vanilla, honey, and cinnamon. Add the tea bag and allow to steep for up to 3 minutes.

Serve with foamy milk as the topping or by itself. This can also be done in the microwave. Double or triple as you will!

Fall Harvest Celebration

Fall is my favorite season, though I truly love attributes about each one: I relish the calm, restful time of winter and the way the light is refracted through gray, bare-limbed pecan groves onto shiny green rye grass in Southern orchards. Spring is newly purposed and forgiving, and summertime is hallmarked by produce and childhood memories.

For my sisters and me, fall, as children, meant hayrides at the farm, the fair, the magic and mystery of Halloween, a riot of colors along the wooded ridge and creek bottom and fencerows, Auburn football games and a sense of relief that comes after the feverish summertime. Cotton fields beguile your eyes into thinking that snow fell upon Southern fields. A humid haze unveils the sky and a brilliant blue forces the chartreuse soybean fields to glow against the red clay and loamy fields.

For me, where fall is only more enchanting, invigorating, nostalgic and relished is in the mountains. Every autumn, our parents took my sisters and me on a fall break jaunt to the mountains. We would gaze on the grandeur of the leaves changing across Appalachia, buy pumpkins unlike the typical orange globes we had at home, eat a dozen different apples with flavors distinct and crisp, and wear our favorite flannels and boots after months of a summertime uniform of bathing suits and tee-shirts and bare feet.

Everything seems richer about fall: the colors, flavors, textures and the intangible element of cool air sweetened by falling foliage, hay-scented fern, baked apples and tea olive—all laced with the warmth of tobacco, wood fire and barbeque. Fall is a collision of all my favorite things—a cornucopia of all that I delight in and cherish—food, family, colors, climate and a sense of relief and peace after the long, hot summer.

The idea for Fall Harvest Celebration in Cashiers was reason enough to make my heart flutter and my appetite wax. To have this dinner with my friend and chef extraordinaire Jason Whitaker was icing on the cake—more so, the rosemary in the ice cream. I hope y'all enjoy this celebration of my favorite season with its colors, bounty, flavors and scenes.

MENU

Mimi's Apple Butter

Honey Butter Biscuits

Sweet Potato Biscuits

Herb-Crusted
Pork Tenderloin

Citrus and Farro
Salad with Pistachios

Potage of Autumn
Vegetables with Pralines
and Dried Summer Fruits

Balsamic Roasted Brussels
Sprouts and Roasted Rutabagas

Collards with
Chardonay Pot Likker

Apple and Rosemary
Ice Cream

MIMI'S APPLE BUTTER

Makes about 4 pints

Pilgrimages to the mountains every fall by my grandparents yielded this Farmer with apples aplenty. Pies, cakes and tarts have abounded this time of year.

This delicacy has a longstanding place in my memory of warmth and delight, for Mema, Mimi's mother, would make this, and the smell and taste bring back memories of her. She would fill dough with this apple concoction and bake apple turnovers or fry apple fritters. Mimi perfected the recipe and we use it on breads, biscuits, pound cake or simply as dessert itself.

I take only a spoonful at a time, yet the jar still keeps diminishing in volume. This sauce is that good—you'll find yourself sampling right off the stove and right out of the fridge—hot or cold, warm or cool, Mimi's Apple Butter will surely become a favorite. When the holidays are approaching, jar some apple butter to give to your neighbors, friends and loved ones—that is, if you can bear to share! It's absolutely delicious spread on biscuits. And apple butter is an essential ingredient in my Applesauce Rosemary Ice Cream recipe on page 183.

12 cups chopped cooking apples

2 cups sugar (depending on sweetness of apples and the cook's taste)

2 tablespoons ground cinnamon

2 teaspoons ground cloves or 8 whole cloves

2 tablespoons apple cider vinegar

Add all the ingredients to a large covered pot or Dutch oven. Stir well with a wooden spoon and cover with a lid. Cook on low heat for a couple of hours, stirring occasionally.

Remove the lid after 2 hours and cook down until most of the water has evaporated. Stir often and watch carefully for sticking.

Once your apples and spices have filled the house with their delicious aroma, you may put up your apple butter as you would any jam or jelly, following safety guidelines for canning.

If you don't plan to devour your apple butter, as we do, it will keep fresh in the refrigerator for a week.

FARMER'S NOTE: *Use a mealy-fleshed apple such as Staymas, Winesap or McIntosh; the typical red apples at the grocery are usually pretty mealy. Throw in a Pink Lady, Fuji or Granny Smith if you want a sauce with more texture and flavor; they don't cook down as much.*

HONEY BUTTER BISCUITS

Makes about 2 dozen

Chef Jason Whitaker is one of those buddies that understands my love for fresh, seasonal flavors prepared in traditional ways, yet with a twist for a contemporary scene. Jason and I grew up cooking with family members, learning from experienced cooks and simply getting our hands into the dough! A foodie friend is the best kind of pal—especially when he's a chef in Cashiers!

Speaking of dough, Jason makes these Honey Butter Biscuits that are nothing short of divine! Just the name implies two of the star ingredients! Honey and butter are always used as a topping for biscuits, but Jason's genius for including the honey in the biscuit is perfection. Of course, a light brushing of butter after the biscuits are baked is de rigueur and another drizzle of honey is completely apropos.

---

2 pounds White Lily self-rising flour

$1/2$ teaspoon salt

$1/4$ pound (1 stick) cold unsalted butter, diced small

$1/4$ pound vegetable shortening

$1/4$ cup honey

1 quart buttermilk

Honey and butter melted together for brushing

Preheat oven to 400 degrees F.

Sift flour, add salt. Add cold butter, shortening, and honey. Mix gently with hands until crumb consistency.

Fold in all buttermilk until it pulls together.

Turn out onto a floured work surface. Roll dough around with hands and arms, picking up surface flour. Do not over-knead!

Gently pat into square shape with rolling pin to uniform 2-inch thickness. Cut with dough cutter into squares.

Place biscuits touching onto a greased pan.

Cook for 10 to 12 minutes, or until golden brown. Brush with melted butter and honey mixture as soon as removed from the oven.

SWEET POTATO BISCUITS

Makes about a baker's dozen

Stripling's, now in several Georgia towns, sells these frozen! I can't pass by there without stocking up on a few. The homemade version is easy too! I love them with salty country ham, Stripling's sausage or various preserves, jams and jellies.

2 cups cooked, mashed sweet potato

2 cups all-purpose flour

1 tablespoon butter

1 tablespoon sugar

Scant teaspoon salt

1/4 teaspoon baking soda

1/2 cup or so buttermilk

Preheat oven to 400 degrees F and grease two baking sheets.

Mix everything together except the buttermilk. Add buttermilk until a soft dough forms. The dough will be *very* sticky! Coat your hands liberally with flour and lightly toss the dough back and forth by hand as to lightly coat the dough in flour. Just don't overwork it.

On a well-floured surface, roll out the dough to about 1/2 inch thickness and cut with a floured 2- to 3-inch biscuit cutter. Place on baking sheets and cook for about 15 minutes, or until the tops are slightly browned.

HERB-CRUSTED PORK TENDERLOIN

Pork tenderloin is my "go-to" meat for dinner parties, buffets and feeding folks. Pork is mild and naturally sweet and pairs so well with a multitude of other flavors. Often times, I like to break away from a marinade and use a crust for the flavor injection to complement the natural flavor of the tenderloin. A crust simply constituted of salt, pepper, herbs and spices is all you need. A quick searing and then finishing the tenderloin on the grill or in the oven does all the work for you by locking in the moisture, caramelizing the flavors in the crust and even making it a handsome, good-looking entrée as well! Taking handfuls of herbs from the garden—especially during late summer and fall and before the first frost—is a great way to bring the garden to the table!

I like to serve a main dish like this tenderloin surrounded by its accompanying sides. One big platter brought to the table or placed on the buffet or sideboard, and you have set a visual feast before even taking your first bite!

---

2 pork tenderloins (3 pounds each, cut in half lengthwise)

3 tablespoons olive oil

2 tablespoons sea salt

2 tablespoons fresh cracked black pepper

1 cup chopped parsley

1/2 cup chopped rosemary

1/2 cup chopped sage

2 tablespoons fresh thyme

Preheat the oven to 400 degrees F.

Pat dry the pork tenderloins and drizzle with the olive oil, coating thoroughly. Liberally sprinkle with salt and pepper and then roll the tenderloin in the chopped herbs, dredging it. The salt and pepper are the crunch of your crust and the herbs are the flavorful essence.

In a searing-hot iron skillet on the range or stovetop, sear each side of the tenderloin for

2 minutes, then finish off the tenderloins in the oven until desired doneness is achieved. (A smaller tenderloin like these can take 10 to 15 minutes; an internal temperature of 145 degrees is a safe gauge.)

Remove from oven and allow to rest for another 10 to 15 minutes; the temperature will rise a little before the meat begins to cool.

CITRUS AND FARRO SALAD WITH PISTACHIOS

Serves 4

I love to serve grain salads for lunch or dinner, with or without meat and always injected with fresh seasonal flavors. Grains like farro are almost nutty in flavor and have great texture. That they can be served warm or cold, with savory or sweet elements, as fillers in soups or as main ingredients in salads and sides is a true testament to their longstanding history as a first food for civilization.

I crave grainy salad especially in the fall and winter. Whether I'm pairing them with some of the season's first citrus from Florida or making a soup with winter greens, I look forward to these dishes with delight. Nutritionally, they provide fiber, protein, little to no fat and plenty of carbohydrates for energy. Adding doses of vitamin-rich citrus only makes this meal that much more enjoyable—besides the fact that it is beautiful too! I hope y'all enjoy this flavor combo as much as I do!

---

2 cups pre-cooked or quick-cooking farro

4 cups chicken stock, or 2 cups stock and 2 cups water

2 tablespoons butter

Salt and pepper

3/4 cup olive oil, plus more for drizzling, divided

1/4 cup toasted and lightly salted pecans

1/4 cup toasted and lightly salty walnuts

3/4 cup toasted and lightly salty pistachios

1/4 cup toasted sunflower seeds

1/2 cup golden raisins

1/2 cup dried cranberries

1/2 cup champagne or sherry vinegar

Citrus of choice: 1 ruby red grapefruit, 1 blood orange, 2 small Mandarin oranges—peeled and sliced into wedges or segments

Cook the farro as directed on the package in chicken stock. Once cooked, add butter then salt and pepper to taste. Drizzle with a touch of olive oil. While the farro is still warm, mix it together with the nuts, seeds, raisins, and cranberries.

In a lidded Mason jar, shake together the 3/4 cup oil and the vinegar with a dash of salt and pepper. This is the dressing for the salad and you can add as much or little as you like.

Top the salad with segments of citrus and serve.

FARMER'S NOTE: I also like to use other dried fruits in this dish. Dried blueberries, apples and figs make wonderful additions! Pomegranate arils make a fun splash as a garnish or flavor accent as well.

POTAGE OF AUTUMN VEGETABLES WITH PRALINES AND DRIED SUMMER FRUITS

Serves 4 to 6

Somewhere between a thick soup and a stew, a potage is a French dish made from a few root vegetables. It is typically mild in flavor but complemented with an array of accompaniments such as pesto or pistou, toasted nuts, fresh herbs, and laced with cream or dried fruit. A potage is a simple background to let other bursts of flavor shine. It is filling and perfectly delightful on its own, but why would I leave it that way?

The chewy, crunchy textures meld with sweet and salty and dried and fresh. For this potage, my friend Chef Jason had the idea of topping it with pralines to go along with the dried summer fruits and herbs I'd suggested. Trust me, I did not shy away from that suggestion and proceeded to devour a large bowlful of Potage with Pralines and Dried Summer Fruits.

---

4 tablespoons unsalted butter

1 tablespoon olive oil

2 medium leeks, white and pale green parts, chopped (about 4 cups)

1 cup chopped celery

1 shallot, chopped

Salt and pepper

Nature's Seasons

¼ cup dry white wine

4 cloves garlic, minced (about 4 teaspoons)

1 large russet potato or a handful of Baby Dutch Yellow potatoes, peeled and diced (about 2 cups)

1 small turnip, chopped (about 1 heaping cup)

4 medium carrots, chopped (about 3 cups)

4 sprigs fresh thyme

1 dried bay leaf

6 cups vegetable or chicken stock

2 cups water

¼ cup buttermilk or heavy cream (optional)

Garnish liberally: dried blueberries, dried cranberries, raisins, or pralines; toasted pecans, walnuts, pumpkin seeds, or sunflower seeds

Fresh herbs, for garnish

Sour cream or cream, for garnish (optional)

Melt butter in olive oil in large saucepan over medium to medium-high heat. Add leeks, celery, and shallot and season with salt and pepper and a dash of Nature's Seasons. Cover and cook for about 5 to 7 minutes, or until vegetables are softened and beginning to brown. Stir often!

Once the veggies are wilted, stir in the wine and garlic, and cook uncovered for 1 to 2 minutes, or until most of the liquid has evaporated and cooked out. You want a little bit of liquid still left in the pan.

Add potatoes, turnip, carrots, thyme, bay leaf, stock, and water. Season with salt and pepper. Cover the soup and bring to a rolling boil. Reduce heat to medium-low and simmer for 30 minutes, or until the vegetables are soft.

Remove the thyme sprigs and bay leaf. Purée the soup in a blender or food processor or with an immersion blender until smooth. I like to add a splash of buttermilk or heavy cream—about ¼ cup. Taste and adjust salt and pepper.

Ladle the potage into soup bowls and top with dried blueberries, dried cranberries, raisins and pralines. A sprinkling of fresh herbs or toasted pecans, walnuts, pumpkin seeds or sunflower kernels is wonderful too. A dollop of sour cream or a light lacing of cream at the table is scrumptious too!

BALSAMIC ROASTED BRUSSELS SPROUTS AND ROASTED RUTABAGAS

Serves 4

Y'all won't find a bigger fan of roasting vegetables than this Farmer! I love chopping and slicing and drizzling and sprinkling everything from potatoes to carrots, cauliflower, broccoli, okra, squash, tomatoes and just about everything in between—cabbage, onions, sweet potatoes and kale not withstanding!

The heat from a high temperature brings out the juices or natural liquids and sugars in the vegetables and caramelizes them. The typically savory or even slightly bitter vegetables have an ounce of sweetness that is complemented with the salt and pepper. It is not a rarity to have an entire roasted supper at my house—that is, every veggie I have on hand chopped, drizzled with olive oil, sprinkled with salt and pepper and roasted at around 425 degrees until browned edges and slight charring appear.

To add a bit more flavor to roasted veggies, I like to use balsamic vinegar. Probably my absolute favorite vegetables to roast are Brussels sprouts. They have long been the red-headed stepchild of the vegetable kingdom and chastised for being bitter or flavorless or rubbery or simply not good. That's because too many Brussels were thrown into a pot of unseasoned boiling water and boiled until they resembled bouncy balls of no texture or flavor.

Growing up, I thought my father was the only human that liked rutabagas. The smell is interestingly bizarre and always reminded me of something—Brussels sprouts! They have that cabbage-like aroma after boiling, and the house smells like them for days afterwards.

I tried roasting them to give them a second try; much to my surprise, they were delicious! I've even used them in mashed potatoes, with mashed sweet potatoes and with mashed cauliflower! Hopefully, now I have raised the standard of Brussels sprouts and rutabagas beyond their badly boiled precursors. I hope y'all will think so too!

---

4 cups Brussels sprouts, halved

1 cup chopped pancetta or thick-cut bacon

Olive oil for drizzling

3 tablespoons good balsamic vinegar

Salt and pepper

3 cups diced rutabaga

Preheat your oven to 425 degrees F. Grease two or more large roasting pans or large cast-iron pans with spray oil.

Lay the halved Brussels sprouts out on one pan (or two if need be) with some of the halves facing up and some down. This ensures good roasting and browning. Toss in half of the pancetta. Drizzle liberally with olive, sprinkle with vinegar, and sprinkle generously with salt and pepper.

Spread the diced rutabagas on the other greased roasting sheet with the other half of the pancetta. Liberally drizzle with olive oil and season generously with salt and pepper.

Roast everything in a hot 425 oven until the edges are browned and charring begins to occur. This can take anywhere from 12 to 15 minutes for the Brussels sprouts and 20 minutes or so for the rutabagas.

Serve them as a side to pork tenderloins, tossed together as a warm salad or side, or even mixed with pasta!

FARMER'S NOTE: *I love to use prunes when roasting Brussels sprouts. They reconstitute with the olive oil and rendering from the pancetta or bacon and are amazing!*

COLLARDS WITH CHARDONNAY POT LIKKER

Serves 4

Collard greens are a superfood that we often overlook. High in vitamins, these leafy greens are a Southern staple throughout the fall and wintertime and are too often associated with fatback, pork jowl and other fatty cuts of pork floating in their "likker," or cooking liquid and natural juices. Granted, these cuts give great flavor to a pot of greens, but some folks these days scowl at such additions and lesser cuts of pork or even seek other sources of flavor.

As for me, I love to use a great piece of pork that will add flavor and taste delicious cooked in pot likker. "Back meat," or a country backbone style of pork chop, makes a wonderful addition to a pot of greens and is usually pretty tender after being braised. Add a hunk of cornbread and that's a meal in itself!

Another Southern hallmark when eating greens is having something vinegary to douse on them. Pepper sauce is probably the key condiment used for this vinegary, slightly spicy kick. I even love mild jalepeños cooked down with the greens to add some mild heat and peppery bite.

Experimenting with traditional cooking elements and exploring some fun twists on these traditions led me to think about white wine. A beurre blanc, or white wine sauce with butter and garlic, tastes so good to me. I enjoy it with fish, pasta and chicken, so I started thinking that the vinegary bite from the wine in said sauce could be good with greens! In fact, all those flavors could! Add some saltiness from a good piece of pork and that could be a mighty fine pot of greens! So y'all try this—just be sure to have some cornbread to sop up the pot likker!

---

1 thick-cut, bone-in piece of country backbone

2 shallots, chopped

1 cup whole cloves garlic

2 tablespoons olive oil

4 tablespoons (1/2 stick) butter

Pinch of sugar

1/2 teaspoon salt

1/2 teaspoon pepper

1 pound washed and trimmed collard greens

Juice of 1 lemon

1 cup chicken stock

Half a bottle of Chardonnay

In a large Dutch oven, stockpot, or deep sauté pan over medium heat, lightly brown the backbone with the shallots and garlic cloves in the olive oil, butter, sugar, salt, and pepper.

Next, wilt the greens in the butter mixture and add the lemon juice, stock, and wine. The wine will deglaze the pan, which will release great flavor from the browned shallots and garlic. Sauté or simmer or braise the greens for 10 to 15 minutes, until the wine is reduced by half.

Serve warm with cornbread, hoecakes, pork, or sprinkled with almonds and lemon zest!

APPLE AND ROSEMARY ICE CREAM

Makes 4 quarts

Whether it's throwing some rosemary into an apple pie or an apple crisp, adding rosemary to apple cider or baking them together with pork and onions, apple and rosemary are a fantastic flavor duo!

For this ice cream, I've made a bit of a twist on my family's favorite custard-based ice cream with the apple butter. The rich vanilla custard is wonderful with the sweet-and-savory apple and rosemary combination. Making this dish is a labor of love but well worth every step. Serve with pecan pie, apple pie, cobbler, crisp or even by itself, and there's no doubt your family and friends will be asking for more!

1³/₄ cup sugar

¹/₄ cup plus 2 tablespoons flour

¹/₂ teaspoon salt

5 cups whole milk

2 tablespoons vanilla extract

1¹/₂ cups Mimi's Apple Butter (page 169)

4 eggs, beaten

¹/₂–³/₄ cup fresh rosemary leaves (from 3 medium-sized stems), lightly bruised or crushed

4 cups heavy whipping cream

1 vanilla bean, scraped (use the scrapings in this recipe)*

In a saucepan, combine sugar, flour, and salt. Gradually stir in the milk and vanilla, and cook over medium heat for about 15 minutes, or until the mixture has thickened. *Stir constantly!* Add the apple butter and stir into the custard.

Temper the beaten eggs by gradually stirring about 1 cup of the hot cream mixture into the eggs. Then add the egg mixture to the remaining cream mixture, stirring constantly. Add the rosemary leaves and cook for 1 minute; remove from heat. Refrigerate the custard for 2 to 2¹/₂ hours.

In a large bowl, combine the whipping cream and vanilla bean scrapings. Add the chilled custard, straining out the herb leaves, and whisk to combine the chilled custard and whipping cream thoroughly. Churn and freeze as directed on your ice cream churn.

Put the bean pod into a separate canister of sugar and thus you'll have vanilla infused sugar.

Christmas Party

Friends come into our lives throughout the generations. A friend of your grandparents may become your friend as you grow older, or perhaps your mother's childhood friend becomes your friend too. Mimi and Granddaddy had a set of close friends, Bunny and Joe Black, who made it a point to take my sisters and me out to dinner when we were in high school and even when we were home from Auburn.

Mrs. Bunny told me that even though she "was in kindergarten with Moses," she could still be my friend and that while it's important to have friends that are your age, older and younger friends are very important too. I am proud that I heeded Mrs. Bunny's advice and have cultivated so many fabulous friends of every age. This varied group of people is truly a great blessing in my life!

One of my dearest friends is Betsy Leebern from Columbus, Georgia. For years she has hosted legendary Christmas parties with themes, costume codes, amazing food, and laughter and joy shared by all! Sadly, I could not attend last year's party, so I had a party at her son and daughter-in-law's house in Atlanta instead—and even used all of Betsy's silver too! Ha! Betsy is a most gracious lady.

Each year some of the toniest homes and halls in Atlanta are decked and opened for Christmas tours put on by the garden clubs. Kathy Rainer and Tricky Wolfe, my adorable friends and floral partners-in-crime, set the table and decorated the Leeberns' home for the tour, thus setting the scene for a wonderful party! As soon as the last tour group exited the house, I began the dinner for my Atlanta gal pals. For this Christmas party, I was the rooster in the henhouse and loved every minute! Stacey Leebern (Betsy's daughter-in-law) and I share many mutual associations, so the guest list was full of our fun and fabulous friends there in Atlanta. I told the girls we were having a Christmas feast and to come hungry. Our dinner was set amid Kathy and Tricky's festive florals, complete with amaryllis, roses and hydrangeas tucked into magnolia, cypress, pine and variegated holly from Lucy's Market—our treasure trove for greenery, baked goods and garden delights in Atlanta. My talented friend Kim Wilson at Lucy's Market has the best greenery, seasonal treats and produce. It is a must for any event or anytime you're in Atlanta!

For starters, I arranged on wooden boards some assorted Southern classics with a few twists: Sweet Potato Hummus; pickled okra and carrots; pepper jelly with goat cheese; mountain apples; candied ginger, fig and almond cake; and assorted cheeses. My Sweet-and-Spicy Pecans were passed around for snacking and used as accents for the salad and our "in-house" aperitif.

A citrus salad, green beans, and a cranberry-apple bake accompanied the beef tenderloin. Seasonal desserts ensured that no one left the party the least bit hungry!

My friends bring me soul-filling laughter. I love to celebrate the seasons, holidays, life's milestones and everyday blessings with them.

MENU

Sweet and Spicy Pecans

Southern-Style
Cheese Board

Citrus and Kale Salad
with Herbed Orange Dressing

Lemon and Rosemary
Beef Tenderloin

Green Beans with
Cranberries and Country Ham

Cranberry-Apple Bake

Red Velvet Trifle

Snowflake Coconut Cake

SWEET-AND-SPICY PECANS

Makes 7 cups plus

As the pecans begin to fall in late autumn across the South, we are always looking for ways to include them in our dishes, holiday parties and even snacks. These pecans mixed with walnuts, cashews and almonds are great as a pass-around starter with cheese straws, as an accent on salads or steamed vegetables, or even crumbled atop apple pie and ice cream. The sweet-and-savory elements meld so well with the wonderful pine-like essence the rosemary provides.

This recipe is a family favorite, and I hope it will be for you and yours too.

---

2 tablespoons vegetable oil plus more for the pan

3 cups pecan halves

2 cups walnut halves

2 cups whole roasted unsalted cashews

$1/2$ cup whole almonds

$1/3$ cup pure maple syrup, honey, or cane syrup

$1/2$ cup loosely packed light brown sugar

3 tablespoons freshly squeezed orange juice

$2 1/2$ teaspoons ground chipotle powder

4 tablespoons minced fresh rosemary leaves, divided

4 teaspoons sea salt, divided, plus more for seasoning

Freshly ground black pepper

Preheat the oven to 350 degrees F. Brush a sheet pan generously with vegetable oil.

In a large bowl, combine the pecans, walnuts, cashews, and almonds with 2 tablespoons vegetable oil, the maple syrup, brown sugar, orange juice, and chipotle powder. Toss to coat the nuts evenly. Add 2 tablespoons rosemary and 2 teaspoons sea salt and toss again.

Spread the nuts across the prepared baking pan in a single layer. Roast the nuts for 25 minutes, stirring twice with a large spatula or spoon, until the nuts are glazed and golden brown. Remove from the oven and sprinkle with 2 teaspoons salt and the remaining 2 tablespoons rosemary.

Toss the nuts well with the rosemary and set aside to cool to room temperature, stirring occasionally to prevent sticking. Taste and add salt and pepper as desired. (Another sprinkle of sea salt is perfect while the nuts are still warm.)

Serve warm or cool completely and store nuts in an airtight container at room temperature. They make great host and hostess gifts.

SOUTHERN-STYLE CHEESE BOARD

There are two main cheeses in the Southern vernacular—pimento and straw. Pimento cheese and cheese straws are meals in themselves, toppings for burgers and grits, and are often passed at cocktail parties and wakes alike. But I am so thrilled that cheese makers and dairies across the South are purveying other amazing cheeses. Their cheeses can be found everywhere, from specialty stores to mail-order options right from the farm. Sweet Grass Dairies in Thomasville, Georgia, and Belle Chevre in Elkmont, Alabama, boast some fantastic flavors of cheeses that I love to assemble as a starter course with drinks for dinner parties and get-togethers.

Taking a spin on the classic Southern starter of cream cheese and pepper jelly, I use a log of Belle Chevre's goat cheese with some craft-style pepper jelly. The combined creamy tang of the goat cheese and the sweet heat of the pepper jelly is luscious with a salty cracker!

Sweet potato hummus (recipe follows), pimento cheese, seasonal fruits, pickled vegetables, and artisan jams and jellies served alongside cheeses from these awesome dairies make for wonderful spreads to start any party. They can even be a meal themselves! A board of your favorites arranged in a lovely manner is the perfect dish to take to a cocktail party as well.

Keep the palate in a state of delightful anticipation for each flavor pairing these boards can boast. Sweet meets salty, with creamy tang against crunchy grit, and vinegary spikes with savory scents and zests too. And, of course, you can't start any Southern party without pimento cheese and cheese straws! Pile some of them on the board too! Y'all enjoy!

SWEET POTATO HUMMUS

Makes about 2 cups

I always like having something new or unexpected with a cheese or starter board. This sweet-and-savory Sweet Potato Hummus is so good with cheeses and other dips. I like to dust it with some smoked paprika for added color. Butternut squash makes a great addition or substitution too!

---

1 pound sweet potatoes

4 tablespoons olive oil, divided

Salt and freshly ground black pepper

1 can chickpeas, drained and rinsed

Juice of 1 lemon

1/4 cup tahini (sesame seed paste)

2 teaspoons cumin

1 clove garlic, chopped

Smoked paprika, for dusting

Preheat the oven to 400 degrees F.

Peel and dice the sweet potatoes into 1-inch pieces. Place the sweet potatoes on a baking pan, coat with 2 tablespoons olive oil, season with salt and pepper, and roast until tender and slightly browned. You can steam the sweat potatoes as well, but I love the flavor from roasting them.

Once the sweet potatoes are roasted tender, scoop them into a food processor and add the chickpeas, lemon juice, tahini, remaining 2 tablespoons olive oil, cumin, and garlic into the food processor. Puree everything together for 1 minute, adding a bit of water or a drizzle of olive oil if need be.

Season to taste with salt, pepper, and paprika. Allow the hummus to cool and serve with pita chips, crackers, or crudités!

CITRUS AND KALE SALAD WITH HERBED ORANGE DRESSING

Serves 6 to 8

A pretty mix of salad greens, sliced citrus, and pomegranate arils with a citrus dressing and voila! You have a fabulous salad!

Fresh seasonal citrus comes into the Deep South from Florida and the Gulf from late fall through Christmas and into wintertime. I love using grapefruit and oranges in this salad, and a dose of some pineapple too. Canned or jarred citrus also works well—the ones packed in juice, NOT heavy syrup. Between the fruits and the kale, you'll be sure to have your daily dose of vitamins well accounted for!

A scant touch of lightly sweetened coconut flakes would add a bit of sweetness. I think it's just about the prettiest salad around, and the flavor is luscious!

SALAD

1 heaping pound mixed greens (such as Bibb and butter lettuces, kale, arugula, baby spinach or any greens to your liking)

1 cup sliced or segmented grapefruit

1 cup sliced or segmented oranges

1 cup pineapple chunks

1 cup pomegranate arils

HERBED ORANGE DRESSING

Juice and zest of 2 oranges (such as Valencia, Blood, Honeybelle or Naval; enough for 1 scant cup)

$\frac{1}{2}$ cup good-quality olive oil

1 tablespoon local honey

$\frac{1}{2}$ teaspoon dried basil

$\frac{1}{2}$ teaspoon dried lemon thyme

$\frac{1}{2}$ teaspoon curry powder

To make the dressing, shake all the ingredients together in a lidded Mason jar. Assemble salads on individual plates and pass the dressing at the table.

The dressing also makes a tasty marinade when combined with a citrus jam for baked chicken or fish.

FARMER'S NOTE: *Goat cheese, feta, and brie all make lovely additions to this salad.*

LEMON AND ROSEMARY BEEF TENDERLOIN

Serves 8 to 10

Beef, with its heavy, bold flavor, is not often associated with the light zest of lemon. Allow me to break that trend and introduce y'all to one of my favorite beef dishes.

At cocktail parties, dinner parties and large buffets, beef tenderloins are often served—and rightly so—chilled or at room temperature with biscuits or rolls and a horseradish sauce. This classic combo doesn't necessarily need a major improvement, but I think the chilled beef works well with lemon gilding the lily, or tenderloin, if you'll allow. Lemon is such a refreshing flavor and is more prominent in chilled dishes. When the beef and the lemon are both hot, then the beef is more prevalent and the lemon is lost.

Using lemon juice as a base for the marinade and cooking liquid, these tenderloins are extraordinary when served slightly warm or at room temperature. Freshly squeezed orange juice with peppers makes a nice touch, or a dab of soy and ginger gives it an Asian flare.

So keep the zesty citrus flavor of lemon paired with rosemary as an option for your beef tenderloins, flank steaks and beef tips. This tenderloin is great for holiday parties, especially when sandwiched inside a good roll with some lemon aïoli.

Zest of 1 lemon

³⁄₄ cup freshly squeezed lemon juice

¹⁄₂ cup plus 3 tablespoons good-quality olive oil

2 tablespoons minced garlic

2–3 tablespoons minced fresh rosemary leaves

1 tablespoon chopped fresh thyme leaves

2 teaspoons Dijon mustard

2 teaspoons salt, plus more for seasoning

3 (1-pound) beef tenderloins

Freshly ground black pepper

Lemon Aïoli, for serving (recipe facing)

Combine the lemon zest, lemon juice, ¹⁄₂ cup olive oil, garlic, rosemary, thyme, mustard, and 2 teaspoons salt in a sturdy one-gallon ziplock bag. Add the beef tenderloins and turn to coat with the marinade. Squeeze out the air and seal the bag. Marinate the beef in the refrigerator for at least 3 hours or preferably overnight.

Preheat the oven to 400 degrees F.

Remove the tenderloins from the marinade and discard the marinade. Be sure to leave the herbs that cling to the meat; these will ensure more flavor as the tenderloins cook.

Sprinkle the tenderloins generously with salt and pepper. Heat 3 tablespoons olive oil in a large oven-proof sauté pan over medium-high heat. Sear the beef tenderloins on all sides until golden brown. The salt and pepper creates a nice crust, and searing locks in the moisture.

Place the sauté pan in the oven and roast the tenderloins for 10 to 15 minutes, until the meat registers between 135 and 140 degrees F at the thickest part. Transfer the tenderloins to a platter and cover tightly with aluminum foil. Allow them to rest for 10 minutes.

Carve the tenderloins into ¹⁄₂-inch-thick diagonal slices or medallions. The thickest part of the tenderloin will be quite pink (it's just fine!), and the thinnest part will be well done. I love the tips of the tenderloin, and, trust me, they disappear quickly from the meat platter or buffet!

Further season the roasted tenderloins with salt and pepper to taste. Serve warm or at room temperature with the juices that collect in the platter and lemon aïoli.

LEMON AIOLI

Makes a scant 2 cups

This is very close to a homemade mayonnaise. I love it as a spread on sandwiches, a dip for pickled vegetables and crudités, or a lavish dip for french fries or roasted potatoes. This is also very close to a hollandaise, which is so good with beef, another voucher for lemon and beef together. Serve this with the Lemon and Rosemary Beef Tenderloin at your dinner party or on sandwiches the next day—if y'all manage to save any!

2 egg yolks

1 tablespoon Dijon mustard

1 teaspoon hot Chinese mustard

8 cloves garlic, peeled and crushed

1 teaspoon salt

1 1/2 cups olive, peanut or pecan oil

2 teaspoons freshly squeezed lemon juice

Splash of white wine vinegar (optional)

In a small mixing bowl, mix or whisk together the egg yolks, Dijon and Chinese mustards, garlic, and salt. Increase the speed of your whisking and slowly drizzle in the oil in a small stream. Adding the oil too quickly will cause this "mayonnaise" to curdle.

Once the mayonnaise is creamy, then you can add larger amounts of the oil and salt and pepper to taste. For a tarter taste, add a bit more lemon juice or a splash of white wine vinegar.

GREEN BEANS WITH CRANBERRIES AND COUNTRY HAM

Serves 6

All festive in green and red, this dish just looks like the holidays! It is also easy and elegant, thus this green bean dish finds its way onto my table fairly often. I love the tart sweetness of the cranberries with the saltiness of the country ham and the pop of fresh green from the beans. It's a one-pan wonder and could even be a light supper.

1 teaspoon olive oil

1 tablespoon butter

1 shallot, minced

5–6 thin slices country ham

1 pound fresh haricots verts or trimmed French green beans

1 cup fresh cranberries

Salt and freshly ground black pepper

In a sauté pan over medium heat, warm the olive oil, melt the butter, and brown the shallot and the country ham until the shallot is translucent, about 5 minutes.

Once the shallot is translucent, add the green beans and cranberries and toss them in the country ham's rendering. Sauté until the green beans are tender but not mushy and the cranberries begin to swell and their skins begin to break, only another 5 minutes or so.

Serve warm or at room temperature as a salad, seasoning with salt and pepper to taste. The country ham is already pretty salty, so you may only need some pepper.

CRANBERRY-APPLE BAKE

Serves 8 to 10

Aunt Kathy makes this dish every Thanksgiving and Christmas. Some of her friends made it at a party when they were all in medical school in Augusta, and she has made it for us ever since. Very recently, her father, my Granddaddy Napp, requested that she make him that "cherry crisp" he likes so much. Aunt Kathy asked me if she, Mimi, Mama or I had ever made a cherry crisp for Big Napp. I could not ever remember such a dish ever made by any of us in the family. Thinking maybe Granddaddy was just succumbing to old age, Aunt Kathy and I had a chat with Big Napp to investigate this culinary request. Granddaddy said, "Y'all know what I'm wanting, that cherry cobbler you make every Thanksgiving. We should have it more often—not just the holidays."

Aunt Kathy and I laughed so hard when it hit us—Big Napp wanted some Cranberry-Apple Bake! When we asked him if that's what he meant, Big Napp simply replied in his famous tone and phrase, "Like I said, folks, I want some of that Cranberry-Apple Bake." We were glad to oblige!

---

2 cups fresh cranberries

2 cups chopped apples

Splash of freshly squeezed Meyer lemon juice or orange juice

1 cup rolled oats

$^3/_4$ cup steel-cut oats

6 tablespoons ($^3/_4$ stick) butter

$^1/_2$ cup firmly packed dark brown sugar

$^1/_2$ cup chopped pecans

Pinch of ground cloves

Pinch of salt

In a greased 9 x 13-inch baking dish, mix together the cranberries and apples with a splash of lemon juice. Preheat the oven to 350 degrees.

In a microwave-safe bowl, mix the rolled and steel-cut oats, butter, brown sugar, pecans, cloves, and salt. Heat in the microwave until the butter is melted and the ingredients are well combined and resemble a grainy, coarse meal.

Spread the oatmeal mixture over the cranberries and apples; bake until golden and bubbly, about 25 minutes. Easy, fresh, elegant, and great for breakfast, brunch, lunch, or dinner—you can't beat that!

RED VELVET TRIFLE

Serves 12 to 16

Depending on which route you take, this dessert can be a labor of love or fixed in a jiffy. You can either make it all from scratch or use a boxed cake mix, instant pudding and Cool Whip. To me, it doesn't matter whether you are a pastry chef extraordinaire or take a shortcut with boxed mixes; the real skill is in layering the trifle neatly and cleanly in a glass dish! Then again, it's all going to clump together when serving the trifle—but I assure you, it tastes good!

2 eggs

1/2 pound (2 sticks) butter, room temperature

2 cups sugar

2 tablespoons cocoa

2 ounces red food coloring

2 1/2 cups cake flour

1 teaspoon salt

1 cup buttermilk

1 teaspoon vanilla

1/2 teaspoon baking soda

1 tablespoon vinegar

1 (3-ounce) package instant chocolate pudding mix

2 cups milk

3 cups whipped cream (preferably freshly whipped), divided

1/4 cup pecan pieces, soft peppermint candy, or crushed peppermint leaves, for garnish

Preheat the oven to 350 degrees F. Prepare three 8-inch round cake pans with nonstick cooking spray and set aside.

Using a hand mixer in a large mixing bowl, beat the eggs, butter, and sugar until creamy. Add the cocoa and food coloring. Mix until well combined.

In another mixing bowl, sift together the flour and salt. Add the flour mixture to the creamed mixture, alternating with the buttermilk. Blend in the vanilla.

In a small bowl, combine the baking soda and vinegar, then add to the batter and mix in. Pour the batter into the prepared pans. Bake for 20 to 25 minutes, or until a toothpick comes out clean from

the center. Allow the cakes to cool completely.

Meanwhile, prepare the instant pudding according to the package directions using 2 cups milk. Allow the pudding to set up in the refrigerator for 10 minutes. Using a spatula, gently fold in 2 cups of the whipped cream.

To assemble the trifle, cut the cake into 1-inch cubes. Place an even layer of cubed cake in the bottom of a trifle bowl. Top with one-third of the pudding mixture. Repeat the layer process so that the final layer is pudding. Top with remaining 1 cup whipped cream, pecan and/or candy pieces, or fresh mint leaves. Chill until ready to serve.

SNOWFLAKE COCONUT CAKE

Serves 12 to 16

Coconut cake is the pinnacle of Southern cakes for the holidays. We Southerners may be able to do without poinsettias, but never our coconut cakes. Since Florida citrus starts coming into the market in late fall in Middle and South Georgia, a nod towards zesty flavors and tropical pairings in Southern holiday cuisine has been en vogue for years. Whether it is ambrosia, citrus salads, hummingbird cakes, pineapple casseroles or, ultimately, our stalwart coconut cakes at Christmas, the citrusy and tropical vibes truly flavor our holiday meals—especially the special things like dessert.

In A Time to Cook, I wrote about my favorite coconut cake from Mr. James Simmons in Pineview. By no means can I truly replicate his cake (I refer to it as my Mount Everest—the ultimate baking pinnacle), but I can offer a recipe that I find fun and delicious. The classic pairing of coconut with pineapple is just too good to resist. Lemon and lemon curd can work too, but I absolutely love coconut and pineapple! This coconut cake has mile-high flakes of coconut, much like snowflakes piling into drifts. I am not too keen on terribly sweet icings, so the cream cheese frosting in this one complements the sweet rather than intensifying it.

The pineapple filling is superb as a topping for vanilla ice cream!

---

1 (15 1/4-ounce) can crushed pineapple in juice, undrained (you'll need the juice for the pineapple filling)

1 1/2 cups (3 sticks) butter or margarine, softened

3 cups sugar

5 large eggs

1/2 cup 7Up

3 cups cake flour, sifted

1 1/2 teaspoons good-quality vanilla extract

Pineapple Filling (recipe facing)

Cream Cheese Frosting (recipe facing)

1 (6-ounce) package frozen flaked coconut, thawed

Seasonal greenery, for garnish (optional)

Grease the bottom and sides of three 9-inch round cake pans; line the bottoms with waxed paper. Be sure to grease and flour the waxed paper as well. Preheat the oven to 350 degrees F.

Drain the pineapple, reserving 1/2 cup of the juice for the batter and 1 heaping cup of the pineapple for the filling. You can add a splash of juice to the cream cheese frosting too, if desired.

Beat the butter at medium speed with an electric mixer until creamy; gradually add the sugar, beating well. Add the eggs 1 at a time, beating until well blended after each addition.

Combine 1/2 cup reserved pineapple juice and the 7Up. Add the flour to the butter mixture alternately with the juice mixture, beginning and ending with flour. Beat at low speed until blended after each addition. Stir in the vanilla and then pour the batter into the prepared cake pans.

Bake for 25 to 30 minutes, until a wooden pick inserted into the center comes out clean. Remove from the pans immediately, and allow the cakes to cool on wire racks. While the cakes are baking, prepare the pineapple filling and cream cheese frosting.

Spread 3/4 cup pineapple filling between the cake layers, spreading any remaining filling on top of the cake or thickening the layers in between. Spread the frosting over the cake. Sprinkle with coconut to desired style. Garnish further, if desired, with seasonal greenery.

PINEAPPLE FILLING

2 cups sugar

1/4 cup cornstarch

1 heaping cup reserved drained crushed pineapple in juice

1/2 teaspoon good-quality vanilla extract (or substitute almond extract)

1 cup water

Stir together the sugar and cornstarch in a saucepan. Stir in the pineapple and water. Cook over low heat, stirring occasionally, for about 15 minutes, or until very thick. Stir in the vanilla. Allow to cool, but give it a taste test while it is warm! It's so good!

CREAM CHEESE FROSTING

1/2 cup butter, room temperature

4 ounces cream cheese, room temperature

1/4 cup sour cream

1 (1-pound) box powdered sugar, sifted

Splash of reserved pineapple juice (optional)

1 teaspoon good-quality vanilla extract

Beat together the butter, cream cheese, and sour cream at medium speed with an electric mixer until well blended. Gradually add the sugar, juice, and vanilla, incorporating everything together very well.

If you like your frosting a tad sweeter, add another tablespoon or more of powdered sugar or even another splash of the pineapple juice.

Swan House Ball

Serving as the epicenter of the Atlanta History Center's campus, the Swan House was deeded by the Inman estate to become the very cornerstone for preserving Atlanta's culture, art, architecture and significant pieces of history. From gardens to libraries to the living museum, the house itself, the Swan House proudly stands as a bridge between the centuries, linking modernity and antiquity through its classical architecture and reverence for high style and perfect proportion. Generations have enjoyed the Swan House and its campus. From ladies lunching at the Swan Coach House (famous for their chicken salad, frozen fruit salad and blueberry muffins) to more recently as the set for Hollywood movies and events, the Swan House bodes well as the ambassador for Atlanta's treasured past and gateway to the city's future. The Swan House Ball is held each year as the major fundraiser for the Atlanta History Center. Known as "the event" of the social season in Atlanta, the Swan House Ball brings together a jubilant crowd to celebrate the history of Atlanta and ensure that this center for historic preservation, the house itself and its grounds, be well preserved for generations to come.

My dearest friends Mary Katherine Greene and Maggie Staton chaired the ball with the same zeal, enthusiasm and class as any royal event! Only Mrs. Emily Inman could have thrown a party at the Swan House with such panache as these ladies did! Atlanta born and bred, these two Georgia girls still call Atlanta home as women of society taking the torch from the generations before them, calling the charge to preserve and protect Georgia's landmarks and Atlanta's institutions. When this dynamic duo of poise, grace, brilliance and respect for Atlanta's heritage asked me to "help" them with the ball, I immediately said yes. And, selfishly, I encouraged them to return the ball to the grounds of the Swan House proper for a truly Southern "dinner on the grounds."

The honorees for this ball represented two institutions of great merit that seldom receive public accolades: the Cherokee and Peachtree Garden Clubs, both a part of the Garden Club of America and the very network and underpinning for preserving garden, civic, cultural and historic integrity across the country. It was more than apropos for them to be applauded, for their garden clubs helped found the Atlanta History Center and its library, in turn endowing the center with a legacy of highest prestige, distinction and grace.

For the cocktail hour, the guests made their way down a magnolia allée, were received by servers in period garb carrying silver trays laden with hors d'oeuvres and champagne on the rear lawn of the Swan House, the home's iconic façade. Music from a string quartet filled the jasmine-scented air as guests made their way through the home and out again, into the tent for the dinner.

MENU

Creamy Egg Salad
à la Cucumber Rounds

Goat Cheese Hushpuppies
with Strawberry Jam

Cheddar Biscuits and
Sweet Corn Muffins

Wine-Poached Shrimp with Cavier

Baby Heirloom 'Mater Salad

Mixed Greens with Georgia
Olive Oil and Balsamic Syrup

Goat Cheese Croquettes
with Dried Figs

Bourbon Bacon Filets
with Blue Cheese

Buttermilk Mashed
Potatoes with Gruyère

Lemony Asparagus

Angel Pie

Shades of faint celery and pistachio green bunting interlined with cream and white encapsulated the inside of the tent, trimmed with what seemed like miles of Southern garden garland. Nearly five hundred of Atlanta's finest folk donned white dinner jackets and long, elegant dresses for a night of celebration under the glorious, chandelier-lit tent. Tables set and designed by my most fabulously talented friends Kathy Rainer and Tricky Wolfe with Parties to Die For were a garden fantasy of their own. Garden roses, peonies, hydrangeas and fragrant lilies filled the tent with a heavenly perfume.

Silver candelabras, monogrammed linens and classic gold-rimmed china filled out the tables with elegance and refinement—all too appropriate for such a grand setting. My commander of the kitchen, Mr. Lee Epting, is my chef extraordinaire for feeding large groups in classic, prompt and flawless style. Lee and his sons, Ashley and Daniel are great friends of mine and I hold them in high regard for their ability to feed five hundred souls in smooth, synchronized style! Lee and I were inspired by Edwardian and Georgian menus but wanted to pay homage to our Southern savoir faire too. From egg salad atop cucumber rounds passed at the cocktail hour to the iconic Swan Coach House meringues for dessert, the menu was a true testament to Southern refinement and respect for the garden and history, all served with flair and elegance.

CREAMY EGG SALAD À LA CUCUMBER ROUNDS

Serves 4 to 8

Egg salad is in the top tier of the Southern salad hierarchy. Atop a bed of greens, as a salad proper, as a sandwich or served with celery sticks, radishes or cucumber rounds, I love to use egg salad any way I can. This particular version is creamy, with a touch of sour cream, You can add as much or as little mayonnaise and sour cream as you see fit. Served on crisp cucumber rounds it is particularly delightful. I'm fond of how egg salad can be dressed up or served casually. I hope y'all like it too!

---

1 dozen eggs, boiled, shelled and finely chopped

³/₄ cup mayonnaise

³/₄ cup sour cream

1 teaspoon dry mustard

2 tablespoons capers plus ¹/₂–1 teaspoon caper brine

Salt and cracked black pepper

Dash of white pepper

Garnishes: green onion, parsley or cilantro, smoked paprika, or chopped crisp bacon (optional)

2–4 cucumbers, sliced into rounds

Mix together all the ingredients except garnishes and cucumbers, adjusting the amount of mayo and sour cream to the moistness you like. Garnish with green onion or even bacon and a dusting of paprika—just like a deviled egg! Serve atop cucumber rounds and garnish as you would a deviled egg for an elegant presentation.

GOAT CHEESE HUSHPUPPIES WITH STRAWBERRY JAM

Serves 8

Similar to my Pimento Cheese Fritters, these Goat Cheese Hushpuppies are a swimmingly sweet-and-savory song for you and your guests to enjoy as an appetizer, passed hors d'oeuvre or a fun accompaniment to a salad. The crispiness of the panko crust and the tangy creaminess of the goat cheese are highlighted by the luscious strawberries—rivaled only by blueberries, peaches, figs or just about any other jam, preserve or berry you might choose!

If you're passing them around at a party, serving them skewered is a great way for your guests to enjoy them, and even a little pan of cornbread as the serving platter is fun too! Lee Epting and the staff at Epting Events taught me that trick! Thanks y'all!

Oil for frying

2 cups cornmeal

1 teaspoon soda

1 teaspoon salt

2 tablespoons flour

1 tablespoon baking powder

6 tablespoons minced onion

2 cups buttermilk, plus more if needed

1 egg

8–10 ounces goat cheese

Strawberry jam

Fresh strawberries, for garnish

Heat 2 to 3 inches of oil to about 350 degrees F in a cast-iron skillet or Dutch oven.

Mix all the dry ingredients together and add the minced onion.

Whisk together the buttermilk, egg, and goat cheese, adding another splash of buttermilk if need be. There will probably still be chunks or bits of the goat cheese, but it will mix well with the egg. Stir the wet mixture into the dry ingredients.

Drop the wet batter by the spoonful into hot grease. The hush puppies will float when they're done—about 1 to 2 minutes at the most. Remove from the grease and allow them to drain on a paper towel.

Serve hot with strawberry jam and fresh strawberries.

CHEDDAR BISCUITS AND SWEET CORN MUFFINS

Makes about 24

In true Southern style, biscuits and cornbread are acceptable at any occasion—no matter the degree of formality of the event. We Southerners may be in our pajamas or in black tie, but we'll be eating biscuits and cornbread!

I like to serve a savory sort of one and a sweeter version of the other—in this case, these are more savory biscuits with cheddar cheese, chives and a touch of garlic. As for the cornbread, a heaping dose of honey sweetens the batter and complements the cornmeal's flavor nicely. All nestled together in a silver basket, a straw basket or right out of the oven, I surely hope y'all find an excuse to use these two Southern quick breads. They are equally delicious in a tux or bath robe!

CHEDDAR BISCUITS

¾ cup butter, room temperature

1½ cups grated sharp cheddar cheese

¾ cup Parmesan cheese

¼ teaspoon red pepper

½ teaspoon salt

½ teaspoon garlic salt

¼ teaspoon garlic powder

1½ cups all-purpose flour

3-4 tablespoons melted butter

Preheat oven to 350 degrees F.

Cream together the butter and cheeses. Sift the pepper and other seasonings with the flour and add to the creamed butter and cheese.

Chill for 30 minutes. Afterwards, roll out and cut the biscuits with a small biscuit cutter or jar.

Bake for 12 minutes, or until golden brown. Brush tops with melted butter.

SWEET CORN MUFFINS

Makes a skillet, or about 1 dozen regular-sized muffins

Typically, Southerners do not add sugar to their cornbread. That is a custom they do "above the line." But, I have found many a Southerner, yours truly included, to sweeten their cornbread with a bit of honey. I've yet to meet a soul from either side of the line who didn't care for cornbread! You can bake this in an iron corn bread pan, cast-iron skillet, or muffin tins.

1½ cups yellow self-rising cornmeal

¾ cup White Lily self-rising flour

1 egg

⅔ cup buttermilk

3 tablespoons bacon drippings

Pinch of salt

Pinch of baking soda

½ cup honey

Heat an iron skillet to 400 degrees F. Mix above ingredients into a batter, pour into the skillet, and bake for 25 minutes, or until golden brown. Serve hot with honey butter!

WINE-POACHED SHRIMP WITH CAVIAR

Serves 2 for dinner or more as a cocktail or salad topper

I have to admit, I truly identified with Forrest Gump and his best friend Bubba when Bubba was calling out the hundreds of shrimp recipes he knew of. Any good Southern cook worth their grits should be able to name a few dozen! Shrimp take very little time to cook and are the greatest solution for a quick pasta dish, with grits, topping a salad or as a salad themselves.

This version of poaching shrimp is more like braising or even sautéing. But since they are cooked in a liquid (which happens to be wine), I feel safe calling them poached. A dear friend once told me that it didn't really matter if I called these poached, sautéed or braised—as long as there was wine involved! I love a buttery Chardonnay for this recipe!

---

4 tablespoons (¼ stick) butter

2 tablespoons olive oil

1 shallot, finely chopped

1 clove garlic, minced

About 1 pound of shrimp, shells removed and deveined

Half a bottle of good, buttery Chardonnay

Good caviar, for garnish

Sliced lemon, for a spritz of juice and garnish

Salt and pepper

In a large skillet, heat the butter with the olive oil and lightly brown the shallot and garlic. This won't take too long, since they're finely chopped and minced. Add the shrimp and stir to coat.

Add the wine and poach shrimp in the liquid for about 3 minutes, or until perfectly pink. Remove shrimp and allow the wine to reduce. This is an excellent sauce for pasta.

Serve the shrimp with a generous dollop of caviar atop a lemon round for a very elegant presentation or as a side to a fresh salad or pasta dish. Also, you may serve this dish in traditional caviar fashion on toasted rounds or bellinis.

BABY HEIRLOOM 'MATER SALAD

Serves 4 to 6

A simple salad of baby heirloom tomatoes, cherry tomatoes and all different types of 'maters, for that matter, is elegant, fresh and lovely. There are so many varieties of scrumptious heirloom, garden and old-fashioned tomatoes that it's hard to go wrong! I love to mix various colors and sizes for texture, shape and contrast. Dressed simply with a touch of olive oil, a tomato salad is quite good on its own or a delectable side with greens, atop a piece of chicken or fish or mixed together with pasta.

2 pints baby heirloom, cherry, or other small tomatoes

2 tablespoons grated sweet onion

Good olive oil

Good vinegar (e.g., champagne or white balsamic)

Slice the baby 'maters in half and toss with the other ingredients.

MIXED GREENS WITH GEORGIA OLIVE OIL AND BALSAMIC SYRUP

Serves 3 to 4

This could not be an easier salad! To me, it is all about the greens and how you mix them. I like using microgreens for their spiciness, with arugula and sweet, buttery Bibb lettuce. Throw in some crunch from some Romaine, some toothy spinach or a bit of savory freshness from basil or mint leaves. Toss with Georgia Olive Farms olive oil and some Balsamic Syrup, and y'all have the bedrock for a sensational salad.

3-4 cups mixed greens (microgreens, arugula, Bibb lettuce, Romaine, spinach, basil or mint)

¼ cup good olive oil

Salt and black pepper

1 cup balsamic vinegar

Garden-fresh accompaniments (e.g., tomato, cucumber, bell pepper)

Wash and dry the greens and toss with olive oil, salt, and pepper in a large bowl or salad server.

Over medium heat, reduce the balsamic vinegar until it becomes thick and is reduced by about half.

Drizzle this over the mixed greens and toss the salad. Serve with heirloom tomatoes or just about anything you desire with your salad!

GOAT CHEESE CROQUETTES WITH DRIED FIGS

Makes 6 to 10

Salmon croquettes are a staple in the South. Often served as the meat for "meat and three" meals, salmon croquettes are one of my all-time favorite dishes. Mrs. Mary makes the best salmon croquettes and Mimi often served hers with grits—and we had them for just about any meal!

A croquette doesn't always have to be salmon. There's no denying my love for goat cheese, and this is fun way to enjoy it—especially topped with dried figs!

1 (12 ounce) log goat cheese

4 eggs

1 tablespoon milk

2 cups bread crumbs, panko, or processed crackers

Canola or peanut oil for deep-frying

3–5 dried figs sliced lengthwise, for garnish

Roll pieces of the goat cheese into croquette-sized rounds or ovals, about 1 inch in diameter. After shaping the croquettes, place them on a waxed paper–lined tray and freeze overnight.

Make an egg wash by beating the eggs together with the milk, and pour the wash into a shallow bowl. This is your "wet." Then place 2 cups of bread crumbs in another shallow bowl. This is your "dry." You'll always have a wet and dry when frying Southern style! Dip frozen cheese balls into the egg wash and then into the bread crumbs and return to the tray.

Heat oil in a deep, heavy-bottomed skillet to 350 degrees F.

Fry croquettes immediately after coating in crumbs, or place in the freezer again until ready to fry. I find that returning them to the freezer for a few minutes is helpful. Fry in small batches (6 to 8) until golden brown (usually 5 minutes).

Serve with a dried fig on top of the croquette—you can hardly beat the combo of goat cheese and figs! Yum, y'all!

FARMER'S NOTE: *One of my favorite seafood restaurants is Jim Shaw's in Macon, Georgia. Their Pimento Cheese Fritters with Pepper Jelly is to die for! You can substitute the goat cheese in this recipe for pimento cheese and serve with pepper jelly—sweet heat meets savory fried cheese. What's not to love!*

BOURBON BACON FILETS WITH BLUE CHEESE

Serves 6

Bourbon and bacon—some things were just meant to be together! This dynamic duo paired with beef filets is sumptuous, hearty, elegant and a crowd pleaser. You can serve this at the hunting camp, lake house, farm dinner or black tie gala— and that versatility is such an admirable trait!

Growing up on a cattle farm, I knew two things for sure: don't get too attached to a cow if you like steak, and the difference between grass-fed, well-raised beef and tasteless meat. "You are what you eat" goes the same for what "what you eat" is eating!

MARINADE

1/4 cup soy sauce

1/4 cup Worcestershire sauce

6 cloves garlic, smashed

2 cups good Kentucky bourbon

Pinch of brown sugar

1/2 teaspoon black pepper

6 (8-ounce) beef filets

12 strips bacon

Salt and black pepper

6 pats butter

1/2 cup blue cheese crumbles

Whisk together the marinade. Wrap the filets in bacon around their edges and allow them to marinate for about 1 hour, or overnight if possible.

Remove the filets from the marinade and sprinkle with salt and pepper on both sides.

Preheat oven to 400 degrees F.

In a lightly greased and well-heated iron skillet, brown the top and bottom sides of the filets for up to 2 minutes, depending on thickness. They'll be a good medium after browning in the skillet.

Place a pat of butter atop each filet with a sprinkle of blue cheese, and tent with foil. Bake in the hot oven for further doneness or to brown the bacon more.

FARMER'S NOTE: The marinade is a sauce for these filets. Bring it to a rolling boil and reduce by a third.

BUTTERMILK MASHED POTATOES WITH GRUYÈRE

Serves 8

Creamy and slightly tangy, this version of mashed potatoes is hearty and holds up well to a robust filet, is a good base for a shepherd's pie or stands as a classic comfort food.

"Potatoes are like grits," Mimi said. "If you don't salt them well in the beginning, you'll never get them right in the end." I'd watch Mimi peel and slice potatoes and magically transform them from starchy slices into mile-high mashed and whipped, seasoned perfectly as a side to many a dish—country fried steak, in particular. Her mashed potatoes did not even need gravy, but who would ever turn down gravy?

Mimi also made an excellent scalloped potato dish. Thinly sliced potatoes would be layered with garlic and butter and cheese and come out of the oven as beautiful as at any French bistro! I relished the crispy cheese on top and how creamy the stacks of sliced potatoes became all cooked together. This version of potatoes takes a cue from the best of both dishes—a well-seasoned classic mashed potato with a bit of cheese too! You can even bake them in individual ramekins and brown the tops a touch.

---

6 cups roughly peeled and diced potatoes

4 tablespoons (½ stick) butter

1 clove garlic, chopped

1 teaspoon salt

½ teaspoon freshly ground pepper

1 cup buttermilk

1 heaping cup grated Gruyère cheese

Prepare 8 ramekins or a baking dish with oil or grease. Preheat the oven to 375 degrees F.

Boil the potatoes in well-salted water until tender. Drain and add the butter, garlic, seasonings, and buttermilk and mash them all together. This can be done by hand or in a mixer. Divide the potatoes among the ramekins or spread into the baking dish and sprinkle with cheese. Bake until the cheese is melted and slightly browned.

LEMONY ASPARAGUS

Serves 3 to 4

I have a friend at home, Tom Cleveland, who is organically growing some of the best produce in our area, from pecans to peaches to asparagus. Tom's wife, the super-talented photographer Ashlee Culverhouse Cleveland, just happens to not love asparagus as much as my family does. So she is always so sweet and thoughtful to share with us an abundance of asparagus. This is a great friendship, indeed!

When a crop is fresh, grown meticulously, organically and with respect, then the produce is that much more delicious, needing little preparation or further flavoring. Such is the case with Cleveland Organics asparagus. I simply give it a quick warming and sauté in lemon juice for a fresh, healthy side to so many other dishes. I have used this asparagus in pastas, salads, stir-fry and even blanched for crudités. I hope y'all have a great farm source in your neck of the woods.

---

1 bunch fresh asparagus, about 8–12 stems

1 tablespoon butter

Juice of 3 lemons

Salt and pepper

Wash and trim the asparagus.

In a sauté pan, warm the butter until it is melted and beginning to clarify. Add the asparagus, lemon juice, and seasonings. Toss everything until the asparagus is slightly tender then remove from the pan. Allow the lemon juice and butter to reduce a bit and serve it with the asparagus. It's really wonderful over pasta, on a bed of greens or with any piece of meat.

ANGEL PIE

Makes 2 pies

The Swan Coach House is the restaurant and gift shop portion of the Swan House. Here, ladies from Atlanta and all over migrate to feast on Southern delicacies such as frozen fruit salad, chicken salads of varying arrays and the famed meringues shaped like swans.

My sister Maggie had her bridesmaids' luncheon at the Swan Coach House—a traditional destination for many a Southern bride to celebrate their bridesmaids and friendships. Our Aunt Sharon hosted the special day for Maggie and her friends. Aunt Sharon is a most loved and cherished member of our family. She and Mama were the very best of friends in college; their stories from school are legendary and many a Southern beau's heart was broken in the wake of their beauty, too! Their laughter and soulful connection was celebrated anytime they were together. They raised their children to love and live by their faith—a trait both Mama and Aunt Sharon learned from their beloved mothers.

When Mama brought Aunt Sharon home for the first time, my great-grandmother—Mama's grandmother—pronounced that this strikingly beautiful Miss Sharon Bellamy was indeed not just a pretty face, but a cousin, for my great-grandmother's mother was a Bellamy—and thus we were related. In the South, blood is always thicker than water and a cousin is claimed no matter how far back the bloodline traces. When asked how we're related to Aunt Sharon, it is simply put as my great-grandmother said, "Through the Bellamy side, honey."

Mama knew no better friend than Aunt Sharon. In fact, my baby sister is named Sharon Meredith, in Aunt Sharon's honor. To have a friend who loves you for exactly who you are—flaws and goodness too—is priceless. Our Mama had that kind of unconditional, eternal loving friendship with Aunt Sharon. My sisters and I now have that love Aunt Sharon had for Mama bestowed upon us. Having Aunt Sharon in our lives is as if Mama is still holding our hands, patting our backs or simply being there for us.

Angels in the South come in many forms. For us, it is our Mama's friends, like Aunt Sharon. I love the connection I have with her and the Swan House, our mutual regard for grand Southern homes like that one, and the cherishing of our heritage through Southern cuisine and style. No place cultivates all of that better than the Swan Coach House. I could never re-create their meticulously made swan meringues filled with white chocolate mousse, but I can make a dessert inspired by such a famed Southern delicacy: Angel Pie, a Southern-style dessert reminiscent of Mama and Aunt Sharon—two angels indeed. I love y'all!

---

6 egg whites

Scant cup granulated sugar

²/₃ cup powdered sugar

1 cup heavy cream

¹/₂ cup sour cream

1 tablespoon good vanilla

1 tablespoon sugar

Fresh berries (about ¹/₄ cup per serving)

1 ounce or more of semisweet chocolate or a favorite candy bar, crushed or grated, for garnish

Mint, for garnish

Preheat the oven to 300 degrees F.

In a glass or metal bowl, beat the egg whites until stiff and dry. Beat in the granulated sugar then fold in the powdered sugar.

Pour the "batter" evenly into two ungreased pie pans—preferably glass or ceramic—and bake for 1 hour. These will puff up and brown like traditional meringues.

Remove from the oven and allow the meringue pies to cool completely. The tops of the meringues may be crestfallen or sunken or settled, but that is fine. If they have not fallen, then crush them slightly.

In a cold glass or metal bowl, whip the cream and sour cream with the vanilla and sugar until peaks form. Mound this cream into the cooled meringue crusts. Serve with berries and garnish with crushed/grated chocolate or mint.

Acknowledgments

It takes a village to raise a child, and I am living proof! It takes a village to keep this child going, and I could not do anything that I do without the support of my family! Thank you, and I love y'all soooo big!

Family takes on new meaning when you have the best staff in your village too! Thank you, Laura Lyn Coody, Erica Wilhelm and Jesse Noble, for all your hard work, dedication and confidence!

I firmly believe a picture is worth a thousand words. I wouldn't be able write without these talented folks inspiring me! Thank you for your time and collaboration! Y'all make me (and the food) look better and better!

Kristen Scott—*The 2564 Project*
Emily Followill—*Followill Photography*
Kate Belle—*Kate Belle Photography*

Ashlee Culverhouse Cleveland—*Ashlee Culverhouse Photography*

To my friends and family and vendors whose events and service in life gave us reasons to celebrate, thank you! I cannot wait to "keep the feast" through our lives and future celebrations! All my love, appreciation and respect, y'all!

Maggie and Josh Schuyler
Melody Jenkins
Jacquelyn Rogow—*Old Bishop Place Farm*
Catherine and TJ Callaway
Virginia Johnson and the staff at Onward Reserve
Jane and Phil Humann
Debbie Felker
Kathy and Gerry Brantley
Meredith Farmer
Megan Brent—*Perfect Pear Catering*
Frances "Susie" Williams
Brenda and Albert Simon
Jess and Matt Margeson
Frou Frou Studio—*Jess Margeson and Angie Brown*
Courtney and Logan Patton—*The Reserve at Oakbowery*
Cindy Keith—*"A Little Something Extra" Catering*

Melanie and Parker Duffey—*The Event Group*
Mary Louise Kennedy—*Calligraphy*
Olive Paper—*Invitations*
The Brokers—*Bill Loosier and Seth Snider*
Maggie and David Griffin—*Maggie Griffin Design*
Joni and Randy Coody
Two Crazy Cookies
Jan McCord—*catering and cakes*
Jesse and Roy Noble
Wilson's Bakery—*Warner Robins, Georgia*
Sara Jo McLean—*The Drugstore Deli, Byron, Georgia*
Reverend Virginia Monroe
Church of the Good Shepherd—*Cashiers, North Carolina*
Mountain Party Tents—*Cashiers, North Carolina*
Cindy and Richard Moore

Chef Jason Whitaker
Chef Jason Willis
The Chattooga Club
Maggie and Zach Yelton and Baby Napp
Kristen and Matt Scott
Amy and Chris Arnold
Stacey and Don Leebern
Betsy Leebern
Mary Katherine Greene
Maggie Stanton
Kim Wilson—*Lucy's Market*
Parties To Die For—*Kathy Rainer and Tricky Wolfe*
Wm. Lamb and Son—*The Plantation China*
Katherine Hoogerwerf—*The Atlanta History Center*
Lee, Daniel and Ashley Epting—*Epting Events, Athens, Georgia*
Glenda Swan—*menus calligraphy*
Jenna Bush Hager

Index

METRIC CONVERSION CHART

Volume Measurements

U.S.	Metric
1 teaspoon	5 ml
1 tablespoon	15 ml
¼ cup	60 ml
⅓ cup	75 ml
½ cup	125 ml
⅔ cup	150 ml
¾ cup	175 ml
1 cup	250 ml

Weight Measurements

U.S.	Metric
½ ounce	15 g
1 ounce	30 g
3 ounces	90 g
4 ounces	115 g
8 ounces	225 g
12 ounces	350 g
1 pound	450 g
2¼ pounds	1 kg

Temperature Conversion

Fahrenheit	Celsius
250	120
300	150
325	160
350	180
375	190
400	200
425	220
450	230